BAKING HACKS

BAKING HACKS

Summersdale Publishers Ltd
46 West Street
Chichester
West Sussex
PO19 1RP
UK
www.summersdale.com

Printed and bound in Croatia

ISBN: 978-1-78685-216-8

Substantial discounts on bulk quantities of Summersdale books are available to corporations, professional associations and other organisations. For details contact general enquiries: telephone: +44 (0) 1243 771107, fax: +44 (0) 1243 786300 or email: enquiries@summersdale.com.

BAKING HACKS

Tips and Tricks for Foolproof Baking

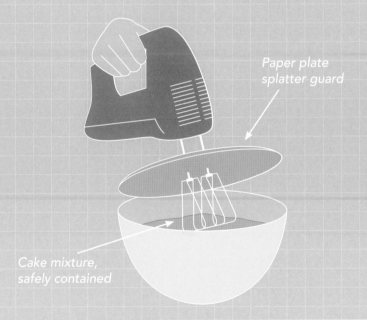

Paper plate
splatter guard

Cake mixture,
safely contained

Dan Marshall

Over **130** amazing hacks inside!

DISCLAIMER

Neither the author nor the publisher can be held
responsible for any loss or claim arising out of the use,
or misuse, of the suggestions made herein.

CONTENTS

INTRODUCTION

For many of us baking is a relaxing pastime – something that we do to wind down and to get a bit creative (usually with a delicious end result). But anybody who has ever picked up a whisk knows that baking is certainly not always a piece of cake.

The kitchen can become a minefield of problems: you run out of a vital ingredient; your cake burns; you get eggshell (yet again) in the bowl; you don't have the right-shaped tin. When the baking stress sets in, what started out as something beautiful becomes the stuff of nightmares.

But it doesn't have to be this way. Enter *Baking Hacks,* the agony aunt of the baking world, brimming with clever tricks and tips to make life in the kitchen that little bit easier. Within these pages are over 130 hacks to help you beat that heart-sinking feeling and make sure that you never feel crumby about baking again.

INGREDIENTS HACKS

A good baker will know how to get the most out of their ingredients; a better baker knows how to make their own in times of emergency. A savvy baker reads this chapter and discovers how to do both in just a few easy hacks.

EASY-PEASY LEMON SQUEEZY

Juicing a lemon: or, as I sometimes like to call it, squeezing blood out of a stone. Thankfully, with this hack you don't need hands of steel to be able to get at the sour stuff.

Place your stubborn lemon in the microwave for 10–20 seconds, taking it out when the skin is warm to the touch (it should not be heated so long that it's too hot to hold). When the water in the fruit is heated the lemon becomes softer and weaker, and is easier to squeeze. The same goes for peeling citrus, generally a messy affair and one that, quite frankly, you shouldn't have to deal with in this day and age. Once warm, the fruit will be much easier to peel. Now, go forth and make that lemon drizzle.

Fruit-weakening microwave

Stubborn lemon

BANANA RIPENING HACK

You want banana bread and you want it now, but your bananas have an unappetising green tinge to them. As it turns out, this is but an insignificant detail.

You can ripen them in the oven. Separate your bunch of bananas and place them on a lined baking tray. Set your oven to 150°C/gas mark 2 and bake the bananas for 30–40 minutes. When they're ready they should be completely black and soft to the touch. Once cool, remove the banana skins and decant the baked insides to a bowl. The heat from the oven will have brought out the sugar in the bananas, leaving you with a soft, sweet ingredient that's perfect for baking with.

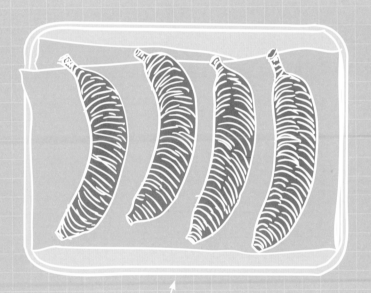

Baked bananas,
ready for banana
bread

FRUIT PRESERVER

Are you tired of being at the mercy of Mother Nature as she browns your apple slices and makes your fruit salads lose their lustre? Stop the march of time in its tracks with this simple hack.

Make a mixture of one part honey to two parts water (there should be enough water to cover your fruit). Chop your fruit, soak it in the honey water for 30 seconds, and drain. The honey slows down the oxidisation process, so instead of browning in minutes, your fruit can stay bright and fresh for up to eight hours. If you're out of honey, lemon juice can perform this trick too, although its effects don't last quite as long.

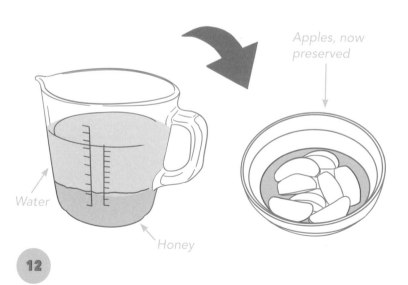

Apples, now preserved

Water

Honey

HONEY RESURRECTION

If you unearth your honey from the cupboard and find it crunchy and crystallised instead of drizzly and delicious, it's not too late to act.

Place the whole jar in a bowl of hot water for between five and ten minutes, and your honey will soon return to its rightful, runny self. This works better for glass containers than plastic ones, but if your honey is in a plastic bottle the hack still works; just make sure not to heat the water above 60°C.

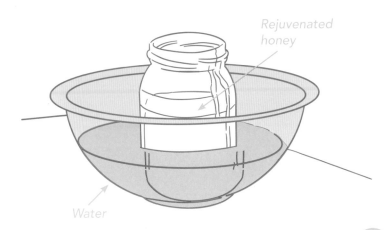

Rejuvenated honey

Water

HEALTHY CAKE HACK

'Cake' and 'healthy' in the same sentence? That's right – replace your unhealthy butter with healthy avocado and guilt-free cake is no longer the stuff of fantasy.

One avocado yields approximately 180 g of flesh, so depending on how big your cake is you may need one or two. You can substitute the ingredients weight for weight, although you might find you need to increase the quantity of your wet ingredients very slightly, as avocado won't bind the mixture in the same way that butter will. If this isn't an excuse to bake then I don't know what is.

Healthy avocado

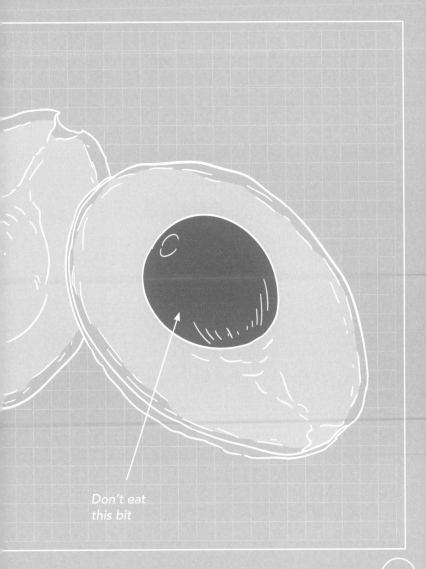

Don't eat
this bit

SPEEDY AVOCADO

Here's a helpful hack if you're keen to try out that healthy cake we just mentioned on p.14. With this trick you'll have your avocado ready in the blink of an eye.

Don't waste time slicing a grid pattern into each piece and spooning out the flesh. Instead, just cut the avocado in half, remove the stone and press each half through a cooling rack. You'll get the job done in one smooth move: no slicing, mashing or mucky hands required.

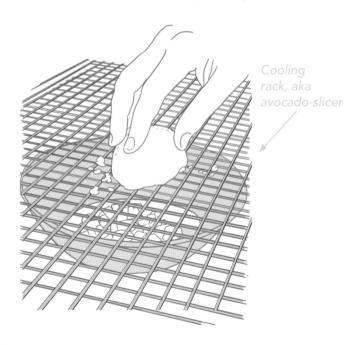

Cooling rack, aka avocado-slicer

THRIFTY CITRUS HACK

Sometimes a recipe calls for just one teaspoon of lemon juice, which is disheartening when you have an entire lemon that you don't want to waste: one tiny squeeze and you'll be left with at least half a lemon that'll go dry in the fridge. If you want to be thrifty with your citrus, read on.

This works best on fruit that's room temperature or slightly warmer. Take a toothpick and poke it through the rind and into the lemon. Then squeeze a small amount of juice through the hole. When you have enough, plug the hole again with the toothpick and keep the lemon refrigerated for later (although make sure you use it within a few weeks).

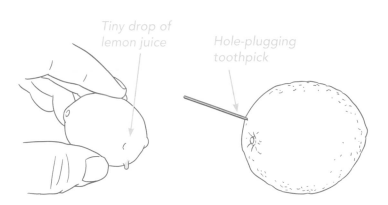

Tiny drop of lemon juice

Hole-plugging toothpick

GINGER HACK

Is there anything on this earth shaped less conveniently for peeling than a stem of ginger? Probably not. Next time you find yourself hacking away at a piece, think back to this hack.

Put down your knife and use a spoon instead. Ginger skin is delicate and papery, and can be scraped away just with gentle pressure from the edge of the spoon. You'll be amazed that you've never tried it before.

Awkward ginger

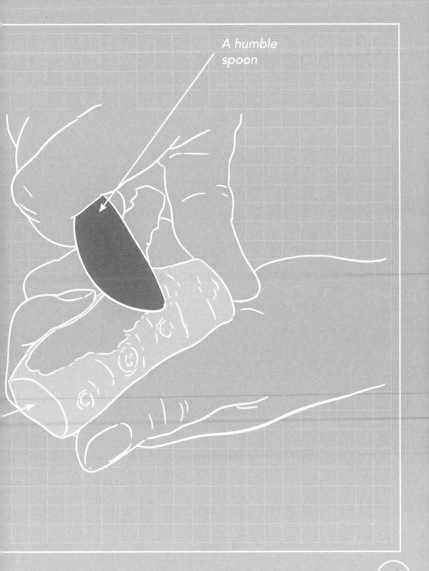

A humble
spoon

19

DIY ICING SUGAR

Running out of an ingredient midway through a recipe is every baker's nightmare. Should you ever find yourself in a bind over icing sugar, however, *Baking Hacks* is here with a nifty tip.

As long as you've got some form of white granulated sugar to hand, you're laughing. Put the sugar into a blender or food processor – using approximately half as much granulated sugar as you need icing sugar. Secure the lid and blitz those granules. For best results, don't just let the blender go non-stop; either use a pulse setting, or stop and start the blender manually. You will be left with fine, powdery sugar. What sugar emergency?

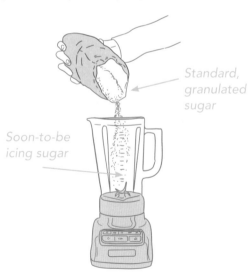

Standard, granulated sugar

Soon-to-be icing sugar

DIY BROWN SUGAR

Ah, brown sugar. The secret to chewy cookies, soft flapjacks and flavoursome gingerbread. Pretty gutting, then, if you run out, especially after you'd promised the kids those delicious, doughy cookies…

Luckily you can make your own. All you need is granulated sugar and black treacle. Put 200 g of sugar into a bowl with one tablespoon of treacle, then beat the two together with an electric hand-mixer. It takes a while for the two ingredients to come together, so hang in there while the mixture looks like a hopelessly sticky mess. Your patience will be rewarded.

Treacle

Sugar

BLACK TREACLE

DIY SELF-RAISING FLOUR

You didn't exactly *forget* to make Mum's birthday cake, you just said you'd do it later. But now it's 2 a.m. on the big day, and you find you've run out of self-raising flour. Disaster? Ruined birthday? Not in the slightest.

You can make your own simply and quickly from plain flour. Just add two teaspoons of baking powder for every 150 g of flour that you need. The key is to make sure the two ingredients are mixed together thoroughly; *Baking Hacks* advises sifting the baking powder and flour a couple of times for this. If you're baking with cocoa or yoghurt, try adding in a quarter of a teaspoon of bicarbonate of soda as well. These ingredients are heavy, so the soda will give your cake an extra boost.

Baking Powder

ALL-PURPOSE
FLOUR

Birthday-cake-saving concoction

DIY BUTTERMILK

Butterwhat? Looks like another one for the grocery list... But why waste time scouring the supermarket for an entire carton of the stuff (most of which you won't get round to using) when you could just as easily make your own?

Just add one tablespoon of lemon juice or white vinegar to 210 ml milk. Stir, and then let the mixture stand at room temperature for 5-10 minutes. You'll know when the buttermilk is ready when it becomes slightly thickened and curdled. Then simply add as much as you need to your recipe.

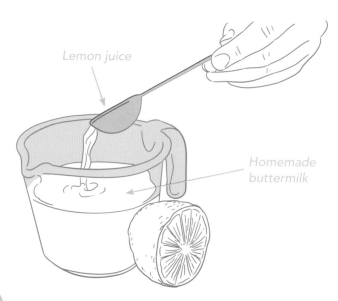

Lemon juice

Homemade buttermilk

AVOCADO RIPENING HACK

Avocados are nature's answer to lucky dip. Will it be ripe enough to use? Will it be so hard you can't get your knife through it? You just don't know. What I say is: you don't need this kind of unpredictability in your life. Bring on the hack.

Wrap your avocado in foil and place it in an oven preheated to 150°C/gas mark 2. After 10 minutes take it out, wait until it's cooled and check to see if your fruit has softened. If it has, go ahead and use it! If not, leave it in the oven for another 5 minutes. Carry on like this until your avocado has the ripeness you're looking for.

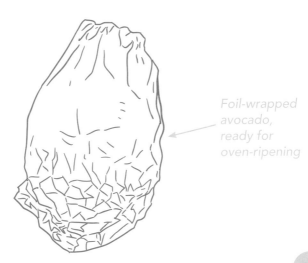

Foil-wrapped avocado, ready for oven-ripening

SHELF-LIFE AND STORAGE HACKS

You don't want your baking powder to let you down, nor do you want your fruit to go bad before you've had a chance to use it. Stay savvy and discover the solution to these problems and more in this next chapter.

COOKIE LIFE-PRESERVER

While it might be tempting to eat a whole batch of cookies in one go, sometimes circumstances call for cookies to last longer than a few hours. How to hold onto that delicious just-freshly-baked texture?

To keep your biscuits from going stale, put half a slice of bread into the tin. The biscuits will absorb the moisture from the bread, and will stay beautifully soft and chewy for longer. Make sure to replace the bread when it starts to harden after a day or so (that is, if there are any cookies left to save…).

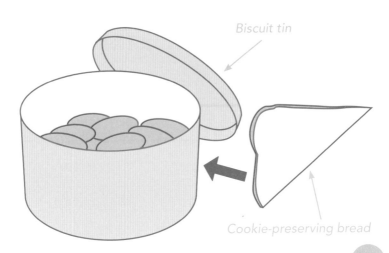

Biscuit tin

Cookie-preserving bread

BAKING POWDER HACK

If you don't have an aged packet of baking powder at the back of your cupboard, can you even call yourself an amateur baker? The important thing is to know if it's still useable - if it's not you're in for some flat, unrisen (and quite disappointing) bakes.

To test your baking powder, add half a teaspoon to warm water. If you get fizzing then you're good to go. But if you add the powder and there's no reaction, it's no use to you anymore. It's time to bite the bullet and buy a new packet.

Baking powder, just before the moment of truth

Warm water

Baking Powder

BAKING SODA HACK

Just like baking powder (and many other things, including my jokes), baking soda loses its effectiveness over time. And if you want your cakes to be light and fluffy, you need to know that your baking soda is up to par.

To test, put a few tablespoons of white distilled vinegar into a bowl and add half a teaspoon of baking soda. If your soda has got what it takes, you'll see the mixture fizz and bubble immediately. If you don't see this, it's time to retire your baking soda from the kitchen. In its weakened state, it can be used for cleaning instead.

Baking soda

White distilled vinegar

BAKING SODA

EGG FRESHNESS HACK

If you're a busy bee with no time to waste faffing around trying to decipher the unreadable use-by dates on your eggs, this hack is for you.

Place your eggs in a glass of water to test if they are fresh enough to use. Eggs that lie on their side at the bottom of the glass are still fresh. If any egg is standing upright, it's still usable but its days are numbered – use it in the next few days. If the egg floats to the top, steer well clear. Nobody will thank you if you put that rotten egg in your cake…

Fresh egg

Very definitely
not a fresh egg

MAGIC MARSHMALLOWS

The next time you find yourself hacking away at a brick that used to call itself brown sugar, reach for the marshmallows.

Putting a marshmallow in the bag of brown sugar helps to keep it soft while it's in the cupboard. In the same way that the cookies on p.27 stay soft with the help of bread, the brown sugar draws the moisture from the marshmallow. The molasses in the sugar stays moist, your sugar stays sandy and you can stay calm.

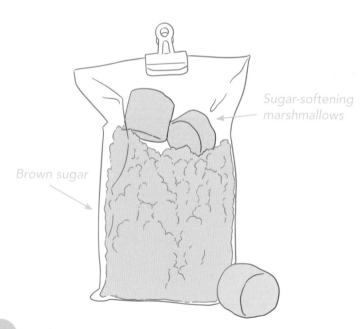

Sugar-softening marshmallows

Brown sugar

LONG LIVE THE LEMONS

If life has handed you too many lemons and you're not in the mood for lemonade, make sure you store them correctly so that they last as long as possible.

If you're keeping lemons on your countertop – stop! Their rinds are porous and not efficient at locking in moisture, so they dry out a lot more quickly than they need to. Instead, put your lemons in a sealable plastic bag and store them in the fridge. They can last one to two months stored like this, leaving you free to use them up at a much more leisurely pace.

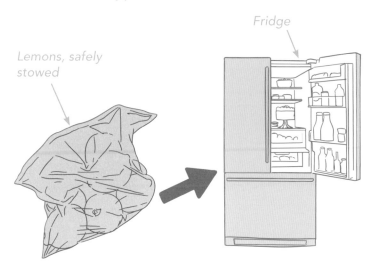

Fridge

Lemons, safely stowed

STALE CAKE PREVENTION #1

If you're ready to take drastic action against stale cake, this hack is for you. It's pretty radical, but hear me out.

Instead of cutting a triangular slice like a regular person, cut one long slice from the middle of the cake. Once you've removed your 'cake slab' (either to be cut up into smaller pieces or to be claimed as one giant slice), push the two halves together again. As you've removed the widest part of the cake, the remaining pieces should be the same size and should fit together snugly, meaning that no area of cake will be exposed to the air. Keep cutting from the middle outwards as you eat your way through the cake. It will be spongy and moist to the last bite.

Cut down here

Push cake together

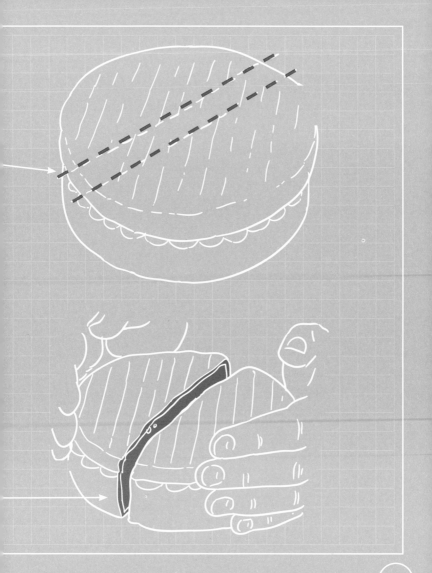

STALE CAKE PREVENTION #2

If you can't quite bring yourself to cut your entire cake in half, don't fret, because *Baking Hacks* has another solution.

Slice the cake in triangular pieces as you usually would. Once you've finished, pin slices of bread to any exposed edges of sponge with toothpicks before putting the cake back in the tin. The bread will protect the cake from drying out. If you have superhuman powers of restraint (or just a really large cake), and you have cake left after more than a couple of days, make sure to replace the pieces of bread when they go stale.

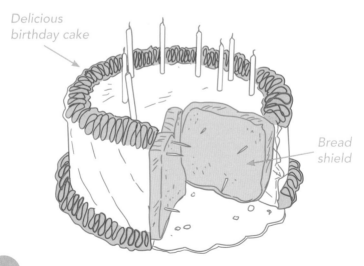

Delicious birthday cake

Bread shield

LONG-LASTING HERBS

Fresh herbs are a magic ingredient for many desserts, but once you've used a few leaves from a bunch what are you supposed to do with the rest? Your only options are throwing it away, or spending the next week wondering whether you can sneak some mint into your bolognese.

Or are they? It turns out that there's a third option, because herbs can be frozen. Make sure your leaves are clean and dry (chopped or whole), spread them on a baking tray and freeze them overnight. Once frozen, put the herbs into sealed containers or bags; they can then be kept in the freezer for a few months.

Herbs, ready to be frozen

BERRY BATH

Berries: so sweet, but so delicate – they are not nature's hardiest fruit. Even when bought fresh, they can turn mouldy in the blink of an eye, and this is less than ideal if you need them for your show-stopping pavlova.

To protect against pavlova sabotage, mix 50 ml white vinegar with 500 ml water in a bowl. Add your berries and bathe them in the solution for a few minutes, stirring occasionally and gently, before discarding the liquid and drying the fruit off. The vinegar will destroy any bacteria or mould spores that are on the berries, and can help to extend their shelf-life by a few days. They'll last long enough for that pavlova after all!

Berry-preserving liquid

Berry bath

KITCHEN HACKS

Ah, the kitchen: arguably the most exciting and important room of any house. Here are a few handy hacks to help you navigate the baker's inner sanctum with minimum fuss and maximum efficiency.

CASE SPACE

You can't go back and change the past. You can't unsay what's been said. And you can't replace cake cases in their packet once it's been opened. These are all indisputable facts of life. Science is still working on the time machine, but until then *Baking Hacks* can at least help you out with the cake cases.

Remove all the cases from their original packing. Then take a clean, empty jam jar and put them in there instead. It will be wide enough to give the cases space but compact enough to keep them tidy.

Cake cases, tidier than you've ever seen them before

COMFORTABLE CAKE #1

If you don't have the luxury of sprawling countertops and wide cupboards, finding a place to keep your leftover birthday cake can be an issue. You want it at room temperature, but you don't want it to get in the way.

As long as your cake doesn't have any fresh ingredients that need refrigerating – such as a cream filling or fresh fruit – try keeping it in the microwave instead. In here, the cake will be at room temperature and out of harm's way (and out of temptation's way too).

Handy, cake-storing microwave

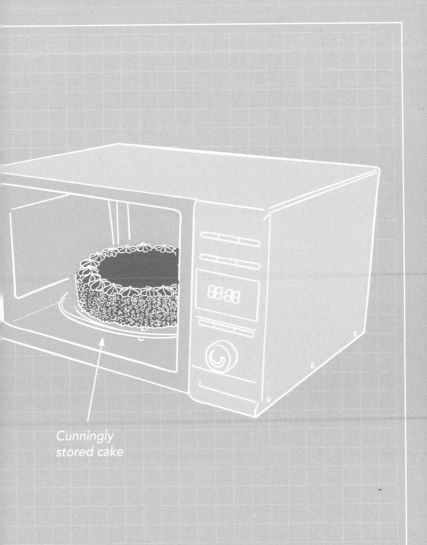

Cunningly stored cake

COMFORTABLE CAKE #2

If the hack on the previous page is no good - maybe you have a custard-filled, cream-topped cake adorned with forest fruits, or perhaps you don't have a microwave - then try this hack out instead.

Take the bottom half of a salad spinner and use it to cover your cake. Unlike a bowl, its sides are straight so it won't smear your decorative fruit and cream. Either keep the cake on the countertop like this, or place it in the fridge if necessary. Either way, your cake is safe.

Salad
spinner

Cake,
squared
away

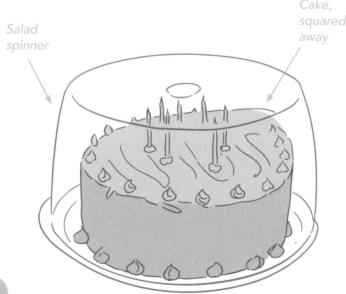

BAKING PAPER BOSS

Baking paper can be a tricky customer, mainly because it stubbornly refuses to leave behind its scroll shape and lie flat. If you've got stainless steel baking trays, then you're in luck.

Take some small fridge magnets and use them to pin down the unruly corners of your baking paper. The magnets will be attracted to the tray and hold your paper securely, and thus order will be restored.

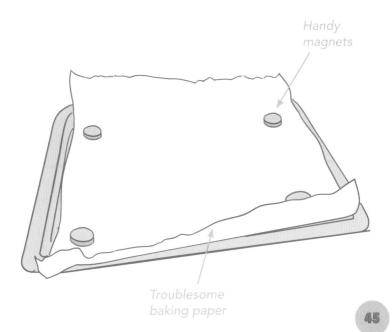

Handy magnets

Troublesome baking paper

STICKY-TAPE SPOON LEVELLER

Any baker worth their salt knows that the key to the perfect bake is accuracy. That means when the recipe says 'one tablespoon', it really means 'exactly one tablespoon'.

To make measuring a breeze, place a strip of tape over the edge of the containers of your powdered ingredients (such as cocoa powder, baking soda or cinnamon). Next time you dip your tablespoon measure into your cocoa, for instance, scrape it along the edge of the tape as you extract the spoon from the box. Your spoonful will be flattened out, and you'll be left with an accurate tablespoon.

Spoon-levelling tape

A perfect
tablespoon

COCOA
POWDER

NATURAL

SPICE SAVIOUR

If you're a baker who likes to experiment with different flavours you'll find your spice rack fills up with alarming speed. Soon the bottles are jostling for space.

But there's a hack to ease this problem. Decant your spices into clean, empty plastic boxes (ones that might once have contained small, hard breath-mints). The rectangular boxes will use the space much more efficiently than round jars, so you'll have no trouble finding a space in the cupboard for that matcha green tea powder you treated yourself to.

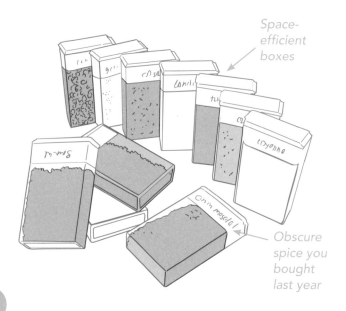

Space-efficient boxes

Obscure spice you bought last year

SAVVY SLICING

The last thing you want when you're slicing your fruit like a pro is a slippery chopping board. At best it'll put you off your game; at worst, it's a trip to A & E.

To prevent any emergency hospital dashes, take some sticky tack and place a small piece on the underside of each corner of your chopping board. The tack will give your board more grip on the counter, and you'll be able to finish your recipe with all ten fingers intact.

Digit-saving tack

Chopping board

SPACE-MAKER

You've got several bowls on the go, the kitchen sink is rapidly filling, and you need somewhere to put your recipe book to keep it out of harm's way. Wouldn't it be great if you just had a little bit of extra surface space to put things on?

Your wish is our command. The next time you find yourself in such a fix, reach for the ironing board. It can act as an extra countertop for balancing your many pans, dishes and trays.

As if by magic: extra space!

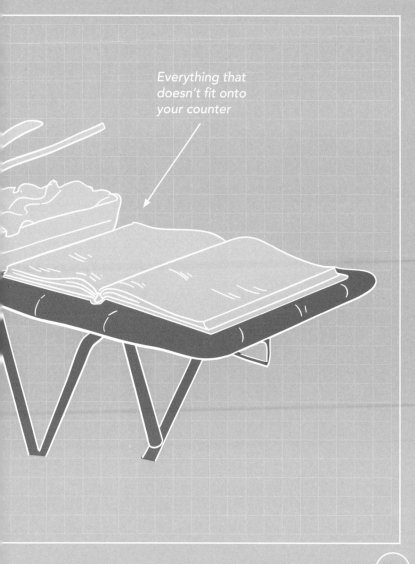

Everything that doesn't fit onto your counter

RECIPE BOOKMARK

A recipe book covered in stains and splashes is the sign of a book well-loved. But while the odd floury fingerprint is okay, you don't necessarily want the entire book glued together because you had to check the recipe with gooey dough-covered hands.

To avoid this sticky situation, mark your recipe with a clothes peg. You will then be able to turn immediately to the right page mid-bake to check the next step of the recipe with minimum contact with the book itself.

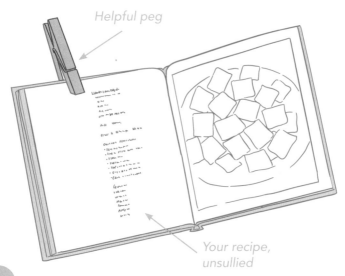

Helpful peg

Your recipe, unsullied

HOMEMADE PROVING DRAWER

Just in case you don't happen to have a purpose-built proving drawer installed in your kitchen, here's a hack to help you out.

Your oven can double up as one to help get a rise out of your dough. Put your oven on its lowest heat for 30 minutes, then turn it off. The optimum temperature for proving bread is approximately 30°C. When your oven has reached this temperature, put your dough in a heatproof container and place it in the oven. Then sit back and let the yeast work its magic.

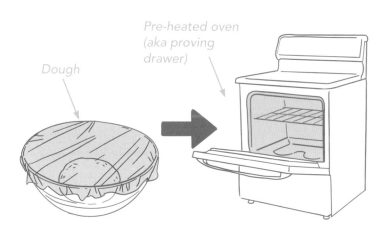

Dough

Pre-heated oven
(aka proving
drawer)

HOT-SPOT HACK

Ever baked a batch of cookies to find that ones in one corner bake faster than the ones in the middle? If this sounds familiar, *Baking Hacks* diagnoses your oven with a hot-spot. A hot-spot is what it sounds like – a particular area of the oven that is hotter than the rest, caused by the air not circulating evenly. There isn't a quick fix for this, but this hack can help you work around it.

Line a baking tray with slices of white bread and place them in an oven that has been pre-heated to 180°C/gas mark 4. Watch the bread over the next few minutes to see which slices brown the fastest, and you will identify which parts of your oven are hottest. The next time you're baking, you can either avoid the hot areas or rotate your trays accordingly.

Looks like a hot-spot here

Slices of bread, half-baked in the oven

CHILLY CLING FILM

I only need to think about the words 'cling film' for my heart rate to rise. Trying to get it to do my bidding is a challenge that I've barely been able to bring myself to face… until now.

Cling film woes will be a thing of the past if you store it in the fridge. When it's cold, it will come off the roll with less hassle, and it's less likely to cling to itself once you've taken your piece. It seems that, like all of us, cling film is best when chilled.

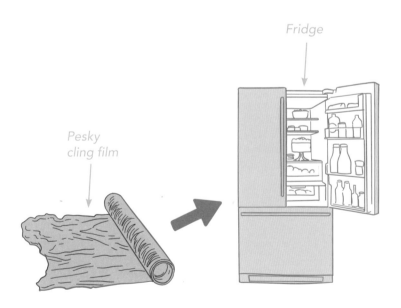

Fridge

Pesky cling film

SHOWER CAP COVER

If cling film is still a bridge too far (and I don't blame you), and you're looking for an easy way to cover your icing or your gingerbread dough in the fridge, *Baking Hacks* has the answer.

Take a clean, unused plastic shower cap and place it over the bowl, just as you would do with cling film. It will work in exactly the same way but it's a whole lot easier to use. Even better, a shower cap is reusable until the elastic weakens.

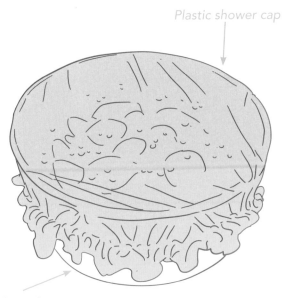

Plastic shower cap

Bowl of goodies

SMELLY SPOONS HACK

Using a wooden spoon can be like playing Russian roulette. Use it if you dare, but you might end up with biscuits that have a distinct aftertaste of last week's chilli con carne.

To minimise your chances of this happening, boil the head of the spoon in a pot of water and then let it air dry. Wooden spoons absorb the foods that they come into contact with; by doing this you will kill any lingering bacteria. There'll be no chilli in my biscuits unless I want it there, thank you very much.

Pan of boiling water

Food-stained
wooden spoon

CHOPPING BOARD HACK

Like wooden spoons, wooden chopping boards also absorb food flavours. Who wants a cake that tastes like onion and garlic? That's right - nobody.

So here's a foolproof way to clean your chopping board to avoid any embarrassment at the next charity cake sale. All you need is coarse salt and half a lemon. First, scrub the chopping board with the salt. Then massage the salt into the board with the half a lemon. This helps to clean away any food particles and smells. Rinse, let the board air dry, and it will be as good as new.

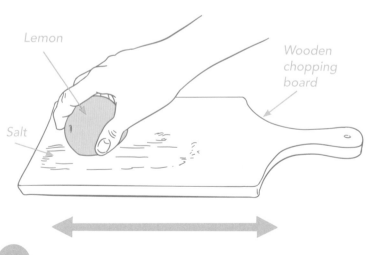

Lemon

Wooden chopping board

Salt

PREPARATION HACKS

Separating eggs, using sticky ingredients, controlling the clouds of flour and icing sugar that balloon out of your bowl when you use electric mixers… Whatever gives you grief when you're baking, there's a good chance one of these next hacks will make your baking prep a little smoother.

SUPERB EGG SEPARATOR

If the thought of separating an egg yolk from the white brings you out in a cold sweat, this hack is for you.

Prepare two shallow bowls or small plates and crack your egg, as normal, into one of them. Take a clean plastic bottle and squeeze it gently, so that the sides are slightly crumpled. Place the mouth of the bottle on top of the egg yolk and ease off your grip on the sides of the bottle slowly. The yolk will be sucked inside the bottle. Transfer it to the second bowl you prepared, and the dreaded task is done.

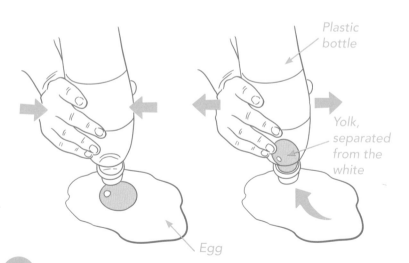

Plastic bottle

Yolk, separated from the white

Egg

STICKY STUFF HACK

It's a travesty how much honey, treacle and golden syrup goes to waste just because it's too sticky to get out of its measuring container. Put a stop to your wasteful ways with this hack.

Lightly grease the side of your measuring spoons, bowls or cups with butter before you measure out your sticky ingredients. The butter will lubricate the sides, and your golden syrup will flow much more easily from the spoon to the pan.

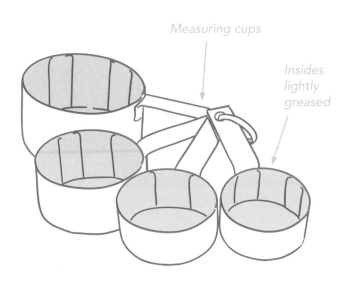

Measuring cups

Insides lightly greased

CHOPSTICK FLOUR LEVELLER

At *Baking Hacks* HQ we're all about finding ways to save you time and energy. If you're using American cups to measure out your recipe, here's a great one.

Keep a chopstick handy near (or in) your bag of flour. Next time you need to level off your cup, simply grab the chopstick and level away. Never waste precious seconds scrabbling around for a clean knife again.

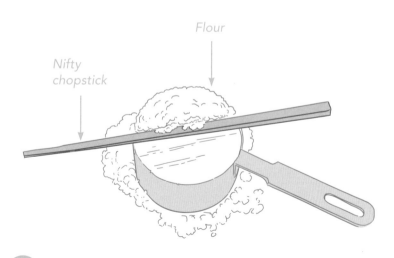

Flour

Nifty chopstick

HAZELNUT HACK

Hazelnuts are great, but their skins are not: they're bitter and difficult, just like I am if I have to try to peel them by hand. Thankfully there's a hack for that!

Boil 500 ml water with two tablespoons baking soda (if your baking soda is doing its job, it should fizz and bubble when added; if not, see p.29). Then add your hazelnuts – this quantity of water should work for up to 150 g of nuts. Let the hazelnuts cook for 3–4 minutes. You may need to skim foam from the top to keep it from boiling over. When you're done, the water should be a reddish-brown. Rinse the nuts in cold water, then simply slip the skins off with your fingers.

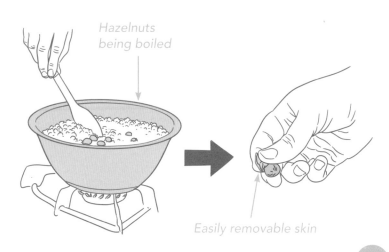

Hazelnuts
being boiled

Easily removable skin

CHERRY PITTER

If you've got a mountain of cherries to pit, and you're armed with nothing but your wits and a few simple kitchen implements, then it's a good thing you're reading this book because we've got the perfect hack for you.

Take a chopstick and push it straight through the stem end of the cherry. The stone will shoot out of the other side with ease.

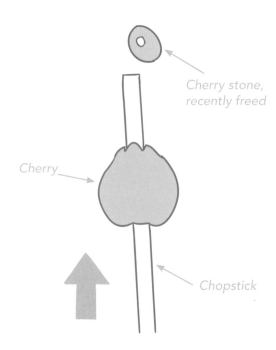

Cherry stone, recently freed

Cherry

Chopstick

DIY SPLATTER GUARD

Using an electric hand-mixer can be messy business. If you always seem to end up with more mixture splattered around the kitchen than remaining in the bowl, you should probably take a look at this next hack.

Remove the beaters from your electric hand mixer. Then take a paper plate and poke the pointed ends of the beaters through the centre. Reattach the beaters to your mixer and you're ready to roll. Whether it's sloppy batter or powdery icing sugar, the plate should help to keep the situation contained.

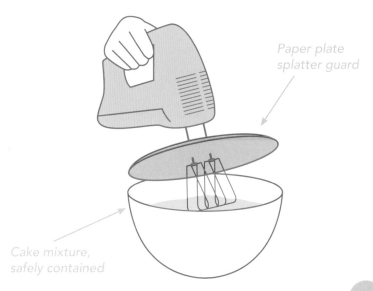

Paper plate
splatter guard

Cake mixture,
safely contained

BUTTER SOFTENER

Butter often needs to be brought to room temperature for best results. But that requires time and forethought. Here's a much easier solution.

Find a glass that is large enough to fit over your butter (you may need to turn the butter on its side or cut it into chunks to fit). Fill the glass with boiling water and leave it for a minute so that the glass can heat up. Tip the water out, and immediately place the hot glass over your butter. In just a few short minutes, your butter will be soft, pliant and ready to do your baking bidding.

Butter softening glass

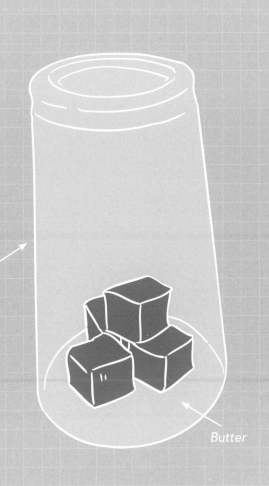

Butter

SHAKEN NOT STIRRED

Maybe you want to save on the washing up. Maybe you like to work out while you bake. The good news is you can do both these things if you happen to need whipped cream.

Chill a large jam jar in the fridge for 10-15 minutes. Next, put however much cream you need for your recipe in the jar (you may need to do this in batches if you need a particularly large amount). Then shake it! After five or six minutes of vigorous shaking action, you will be left with perfectly whipped cream, no fiddly beaters to wash, and the toned arms of a gym pro.

Tightly secured lid

Jar of cream

DOUGH-KNEADING HACK

There is nothing more satisfying in baking than the feeling of kneading dough. If you've got a sticky dough, however, the therapy session descends into mess and chaos before you can say 'active dry yeast'.

Next time you're faced with such a dough, try wetting your hands lightly with water before you start to roll or knead. Your hands should be damp rather than wet, otherwise you risk changing the consistency of your dough. You can also try lightly oiling your hands if you prefer. The moisture will help to prevent the dough from sticking to your hands, so now you have no knead to worry.

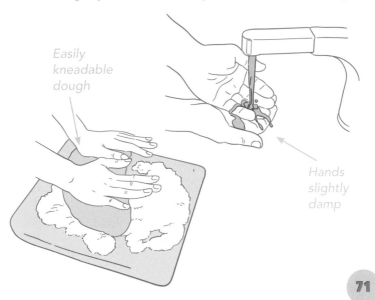

Easily kneadable dough

Hands slightly damp

KEEPING IT COOL

Baking with cold butter is like dealing with a ticking time bomb. Spend too long cutting it up into usable pieces, and by the time you've mixed it with your flour it's warmed back up to room temperature. Useless.

So try grating it instead. Your butter will be transformed into tiny pieces that can be coated in flour in mere seconds. Before you know it, your dough is in the oven with the butter still crisp and cold. Flaky pastry and beautiful biscuits, here you come.

Butter, ready for use

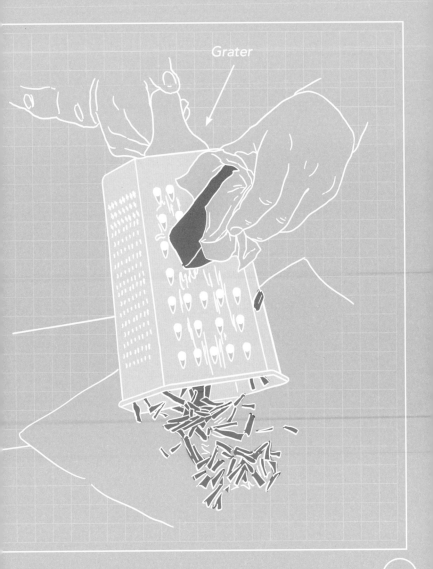

Grater

73

HAND-MIXING HACK

At *Baking Hacks* HQ, not only do we want your bakes to turn out well but we care about your well-being too. So take heed of this next hack.

Next time you're making something that requires a long stint on the electric hand-mixer, like royal icing or meringue, don't move the mixer round the bowl with your hand. Instead, hold the mixer in a fixed position and rotate the bowl, as this is a lot less tiring for your forearms. You can thank me later.

Arm that isn't tired

Hand-mixer

Bowl

SPEEDY WHIPPED CREAM

If you ever find yourself needing to whip cream at a moment's notice, here's a hack to speed things up without affecting the quality of those firm, stiff peaks.

Simply put your beaters and bowl in the fridge or freezer for a few minutes. Once your equipment is cool, go ahead and whip. When you whip cream you create tiny air pockets. The fat then gradually forms protective bubbles around the air, turning your cream from a liquid into the spreadable peaks we know and love. Being cold helps this process to happen faster and more effectively.

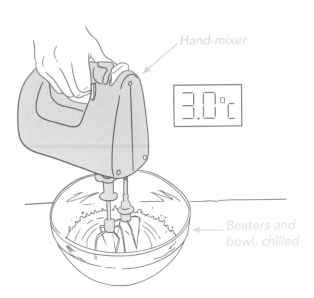

Hand-mixer

3.0°c

Beaters and bowl, chilled

PUMPKIN PREPARATION

Pumpkins may not be the most common of fruits, but when one does present itself you need to be prepared.

A spoon should not be your weapon of choice in your battle to de-seed a pumpkin. Take the *Baking Hacks* advice and use an ice-cream scoop instead. Its rounded shape allows you to cut through the fibrous insides with ease, and it can also catch the seeds as it goes. You'll have your pumpkin pie made in a flash.

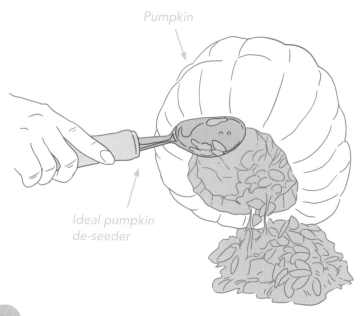

Pumpkin

Ideal pumpkin
de-seeder

EGGSHELL REMOVER #1

Knowing the grief of eggshell-in-the-bowl is something that unites all bakers, from the intrepid beginner right the way up to the most accomplished pâtissier. Banish the pain with this hack.

When you come across a piece of shell trespassing in your bowl, just wet your fingers before dipping in to remove it (no, I didn't say lick your finger). Instead of fleeing, the shell should gravitate towards your finger, and you can pick it out of your mixture with ease.

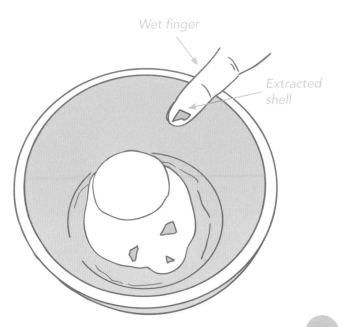

Wet finger

Extracted shell

EGGSHELL REMOVER #2

If you'd rather not stick your fingers into the bowl to retrieve eggshell, *Baking Hacks* has another, more elegant solution.

Take one half of the now-empty eggshell and use it like a spoon to scoop out the offending fragment. The sharp edge will break through the thick egg white, so you can remove the piece of shell while keeping clean-fingered and frustration-free.

Shell fragment, no longer tresspassing

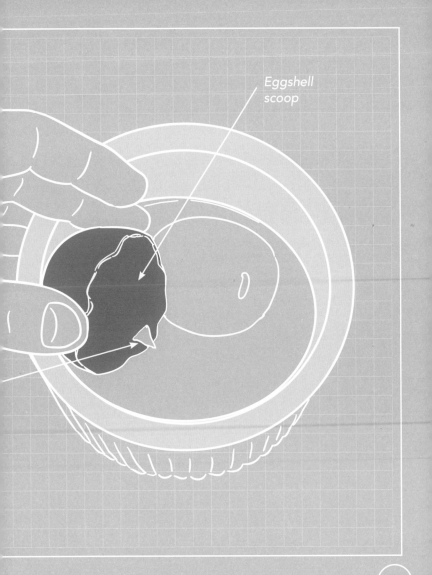

Eggshell
scoop

CLOUD CONTROL

If you don't keep your wits about you when you're using a stand mixer full of flour, you could be in for a large-scale clean-up operation.

To keep your dry ingredients from flying out of the bowl, drape a clean tea towel over your mixer before you switch it on. Whether you're trying to prevent clouds of flour or puffs of icing sugar, the tea towel will keep all of it contained and your kitchen tidy.

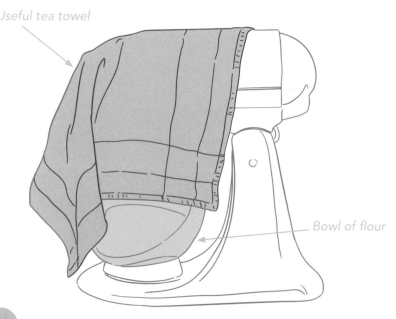

Useful tea towel

Bowl of flour

FOOLPROOFING HACKS

To be able to guarantee the success of your bakes –
that's the dream of many who take up the whisk and
apron. And with these few hacks, you really can. They'll
make great conversation starters too (that is, if you're
willing to share your secrets).

CURDLE PREVENTION

Ah, the dreaded C-word. There's no shame in admitting to having had a cake mixture that's curdled: it's happened to all of us. But we can rise above our curdly pasts – with this hack, in fact.

Curdling in cake mix often occurs when your butter is room temperature but your eggs are chilled. The temperature difference makes it more difficult for the fat and the water in the ingredients to bind together and the mixture separates into the curdled mess we dread. So, next time you get to work on your Victoria sponge, put your eggs in a bowl of warm water for a few minutes before you add them to your cake mix. This will quickly bring them to room temperature and make them bind with your butter much more successfully.

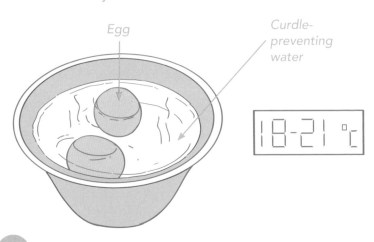

Egg

Curdle-preventing water

18-21 °C

MAGIC CAKE RELEASE

You greased the tin copiously with butter, but somehow you're still having to deal with the grief of a brownie mix stuck to its baking tray.

To avoid this heartbreak in future bakes, beat together 50 g vegetable shortening, 60 ml vegetable oil and 30 g plain flour. Use this instead of plain butter to grease your cake tins and your bakes should come away from the sides with no trouble. As long as it's stored in the fridge in an airtight container, the mixture can keep for a couple of months. Alternatively, just line the tin with baking paper next time!

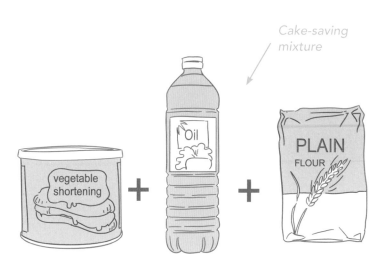

Cake-saving mixture

PERFECT VICTORIA SPONGE

If you want even more tips for creating a barnstorming Victoria sponge, you're in luck.

Before you even start getting your bowls and beaters out, weigh the eggs that you plan to use. However much they weigh (in their shells), use the same weight's worth of flour, sugar and butter (for instance, if your eggs come to a total of 120 g, use 120 g butter, 120 g flour and 120 g sugar). This guarantees you the right proportions of your ingredients every time, and a simply stunning Victoria sponge. The church cake sale won't know what's hit it.

Lowly eggs

Weighing scales

DROP IT LIKE IT'S HOT

If you don't want Doris from number 59 to take the prize for the best Victoria sponge at the next village fete, you'll want to pay attention to this next hack.

Prepare your prize-winning batter as usual and pour it into the pan. Then lift the whole tin about a foot off the countertop and drop it. The impact will get rid of any large air bubbles that might be lurking, so you can be sure that you'll have a beautifully even cake all the way through with no unsightly lumps and bumps. Beat that, Doris.

Cake falling through the air

Counter top

UNIFORM CUPCAKES

We've all been there: you take a batch of cupcakes out of the oven to find that, while some have ballooned into beautiful golden domes, some of them aren't even tickling the rim of their case. It's a sad story for these ones. They'll be the last in the tin, probably forgotten…

But you could prevent all this! Simply use an ice cream scoop to measure out your cake mixture into the cake cases and your cupcakes will come out in uniform size.

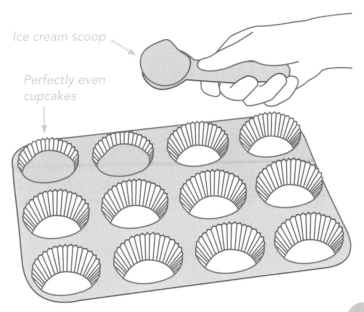

Ice cream scoop

Perfectly even cupcakes

BAKING WITH SPIRIT

You know your mother-in-law will be polite about your double-crusted apple pie whatever state the pastry's in, but it's not a crime to want to knock it out of the park. To get perfect flaky pastry every time, listen up.

The secret is to add vodka to your pastry dough. Begin by adding a teaspoon to your dough just before it's ready to roll out, and then work it in. Add enough so that your dough is pliant but not so much that it becomes sticky. Then chill the dough for 15 minutes before rolling out and baking as usual. The vodka will evaporate when the pastry bakes, and you will be left with golden flakes of perfection.

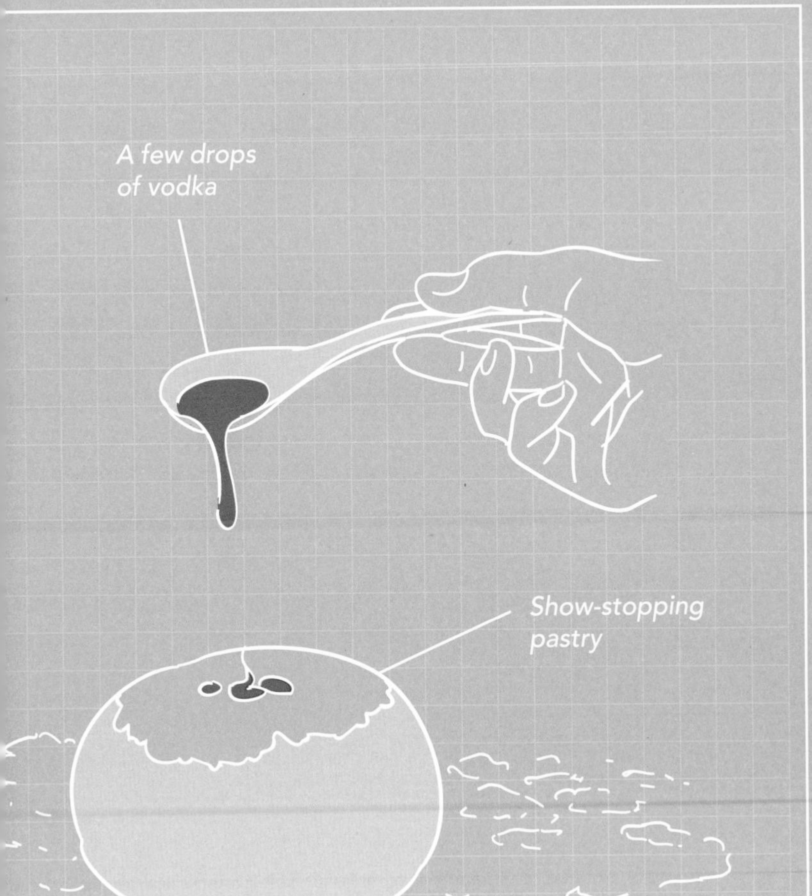

A few drops
of vodka

Show-stopping
pastry

89

BUOYANT BLUEBERRIES

If you're put off the idea of making blueberry muffins for fear that your fruit will sink, take heart, because *Baking Hacks* is here with a tip.

Reserve a few spoonfuls of flour from your recipe and use it to coat the blueberries that you're adding to the mixture. This coating helps them to stick to the batter and stay suspended instead of sinking to the bottom of the tin. And it's not just for blueberries: this hack will work on most things you add to your bakes, whether it's raisins, cranberries or chocolate chips.

Flour-coated
blueberries

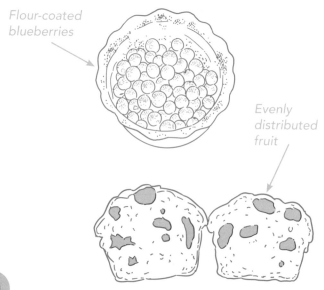

Evenly
distributed
fruit

BAKING HACKS

The bowls are empty, the tins have been filled and the oven door is closed. The fate of your bake is now in the hands of the gods. Or is it? Read on to discover some nifty tricks to help you look after your bake while it's doing its thing in the oven.

FLAT-TOPPED CAKE

If you're tired of having to level off the unsightly dome that appears on every cake that you bake, then try this hack for size.

Take an old cotton T-shirt or kitchen towel and cut a strip long enough to tie around your tin. Before putting the cake in the oven, run the strip under cold water and wring it out so that it's as wet as possible without dripping. Tie or safety-pin the strip around your tin, and bake your cake as normal. The wet strip stops the outside of the cake from cooking too quickly, so the cake will bake more evenly. No trimming necessary!

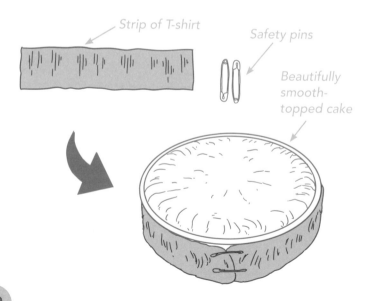

Strip of T-shirt

Safety pins

Beautifully smooth-topped cake

CHEWY COOKIE HACK

There's a fine line between a cookie being chewy perfection and a jaw-breaking endurance task. Never deal with the latter again with this next hack.

Don't wait for your cookies to bake all the way through when they're in the oven. Instead, take them out when the edges have just hardened and leave them to cool for a few minutes on the hot tray before transferring them to a cooling rack. You'll catch them in their optimum chewy state and avoid over-baking every time.

Perfect cookies, just hardened at the edge

PIE-CRUST PROTECTOR

Pie crusts are delicate beings and deserve to be treated with respect. Don't take chances with yours – instead, use this hack to ensure golden crusts every time.

Before putting your pie or tart in the oven, take a square of foil that's large enough to cover the circumference of your dish. Fold it in half then in half again, and cut one corner off in a curved line as shown in image 3. Open it up and you should have a circular shape cut in the middle of the foil. When your bake is halfway through cooking, take it from the oven, place the foil loosely over the top and tuck in the edges (minding your fingers on the hot dish). Put it back in the oven until it's done. The foil deflects heat, ensuring that your pie is baked but your edges don't burn.

Foil crust-protector

Pie-crust: shielded

THE SKEWER TEST

Unless you've got your recipe down to a T, it's tricky to pinpoint the moment when your cake is *just* ready to come out of the oven. Too soon and you've got a squidgy mess. Too late and you'll need a lot of icing to compensate for the dryness.

Next time you're faced with this dilemma, poke a skewer or toothpick into the middle of your cake. If it comes out clean, your cake is ready. If it comes out sticky, then give your cake another few minutes. Repeat as many times as you need until the cake is done.

Metal skewer

Cake, maybe cooked, maybe not...

THE SPRING TEST

If the skewer hack still hasn't got you convinced, here's another way to test whether your cake is truly baked.

Remove the cake from the oven and, with one finger, gently push down on the centre. The cake should depress and spring back gently if it's done. If not, leave it in for a few more minutes and put your feet up while you wait, safe in the knowledge that the cake situation is under control.

Cake-testing finger

Cake

NO SOGGY BOTTOMS

Making a pie with a fruity, juicy filling is a noble endeavour but sometimes it can come at a price. While the taste is supreme, you run a severe risk of the dreaded soggy bottom.

But there is a way to cover your back (or your bottom). Add two tablespoons of tapioca flour to your fruity filling and mix well before pouring it into your pastry case. This will help to thicken the filling and make it less runny, so it's less likely to seep through your pastry and make it soggy. This hack is especially useful if you're making a pie with frozen fruits, as these can be particularly watery.

Bottom,
not soggy

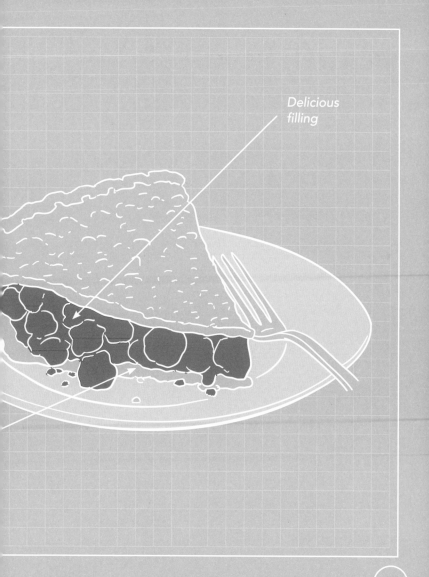

Delicious
filling

BEAUTIFUL BREAD

Do you covet the beautifully domed loaves of bread that you see lined up in the window of your local bakery? We certainly do here at *Baking Hacks* HQ, so we've got a hack to help you out.

Put a couple of handfuls of ice cubes on a baking tray and place this on the bottom shelf of your oven when you put your bread in. Bread rises rapidly in the first few minutes of baking, and the steam created by the ice cubes will help to keep the crust moist so the bread can keep expanding. After 5–10 minutes, remove the baking tray so that the bread has time to dry out and become the crusty, golden dome it is destined to be.

Bread, soon to be beautifully domed

Ice cubes

UNIFORM COOKIES

Even if you measure out your cookie dough to the gram, there's still a chance that the cookies will spread out in different ways once they're left to their own devices in the oven. If you can't stand this kind of insubordination, try this next hack.

Put each ball of cookie dough in a muffin tin rather than on a flat baking tray. The round bottoms of the tray will keep them in perfect, uniform circles. That'll show the cookies who's boss.

Muffin tin

Very round cookies

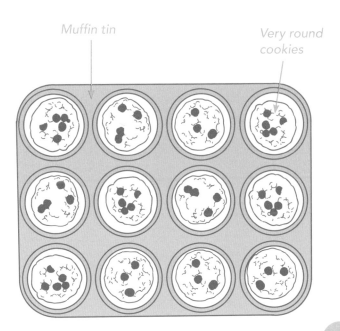

SHAPE-HOLDING HACK

If it's a perpetual source of sadness to you that your plaited pie crusts and your intricately shaped sugar cookies lose their definition while they're in the oven, chin up and read on.

Next time you want your artistic efforts to stand out, put your sugar cookies or pastry cases in the freezer for 10 minutes before you bake them. This will help to stop the dough or pastry from spreading too far or puffing up in the oven, and you'll be able to serve up your treats with pride, showing off their beautifully defined edges.

Fridge

Impressively intricate cookies

DECORATING HACKS

Whether you want to pipe, garnish, or present like a pro, or whether you just want some simple ways to impress, this chapter has plenty of hacks to help you up your game and kid people into thinking you've got some seriously fancy skills.

DOILY STENCIL

Grandma's asked for her favourite plain chocolate sponge cake for her birthday again. You know you could bake it with your eyes closed, but isn't there something underwhelming about a plain, icing-sugar-dusted cake? Not if *Baking Hacks* has anything to do with it.

This time, before you add the icing sugar, put a clean doily on top of your cake, then dust the icing sugar over it. Remove the doily and your cake will be an intricately patterned masterpiece. You'll knock Grandma's socks off.

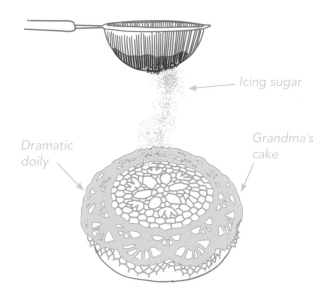

Icing sugar

Dramatic doily

Grandma's cake

FANCY CHOCOLATE GARNISH

If you're looking for an epic cupcake topper, something to spruce up your ice cream, or an avant garde decoration for your layer cake, try this next hack.

Take a sheet of bubble wrap, making sure that it's both clean and completely dry. Melt a bar of chocolate, pour it over the sheet of bubble wrap and leave it in the fridge. Once the chocolate has set, gently peel away the bubble wrap, break the chocolate into pieces and *voilà*: stunning visuals for your cake at a minimal difficulty level.

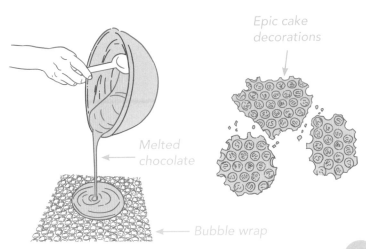

Epic cake decorations

Melted chocolate

Bubble wrap

PICTURE-PERFECT PIPING #1

If your attempts at piping tend to look like a child's drawing that you'd stick on a fridge, then *Baking Hacks* has just the thing for you.

Try putting your icing into a plastic syringe instead of a piping bag (these can be bought cheaply online). Being thinner and more pen-shaped than a piping bag, the syringe is a lot easier to use and lets you get that level of accuracy to your piping that suggests 'artisan' rather than 'amateur'.

Precision piping device

Precision piping

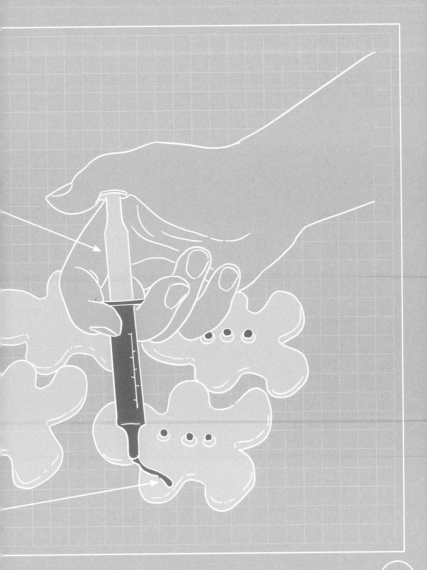

PICTURE-PERFECT PIPING #2

Piping straight onto a cake is not for the faint-hearted. You need a steady hand and nerves of steel. If you fear that you'll crack under the pressure, this hack could help you out.

Instead of piping straight onto the cake, pipe your design or your lettering onto a piece of wax paper (available in supermarkets). Once you're happy that what you've created is something you'd want to see on your cake, put the paper and icing in the freezer. Once it's frozen, simply peel the paper away and place the icing on top of the cake.

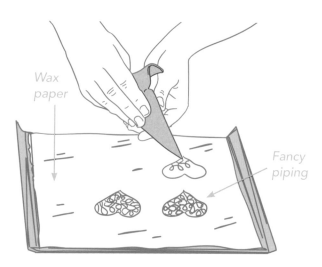

Wax paper

Fancy piping

PIPING BAG HACK

Whenever I'm trying to fill a piping bag I always wish I had a few extra hands. Here's a hack to make the task easier.

Secure the nozzle at the end of your piping bag. Then place the whole bag into a cup and roll the top of the bag down around it. The cup will support the bag and keep the top open, leaving you free to fill it up while keeping the edges of the bag clean.

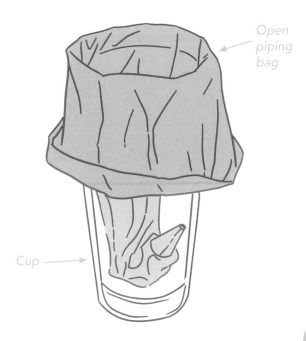

Open piping bag

Cup

FANCY FROSTING

You don't have to cover your cake in piping or fancy garnishes for it to turn heads. All you really need is some cutlery (and no, I don't mean to eat the cake with).

Next time you've got a cake frosted with buttercream, grab a fork or a spoon. Use the prongs of the fork or the curve in the spoon to create patterns in the soft icing: simple, but effective.

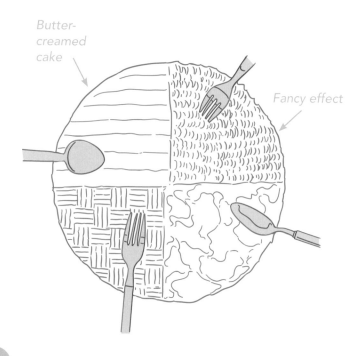

Butter-
creamed
cake

Fancy effect

PIMP THAT PIE CRUST

Nothing livens up a dinner party like a fancy pie crust, so here's a hack that makes it child's play.

All you need are your best pearls. Before baking, take your necklace and press it into the edge of your pastry until it leaves round indentations. Continue round the pie until the whole crust is done, and you've got yourself one classy pie crust. You don't even have to use a necklace; you can use anything that leaves a mark to create a pattern. Tongs, forks, a corkscrew – plunder your kitchen for interestingly shaped implements and let your imagination run wild.

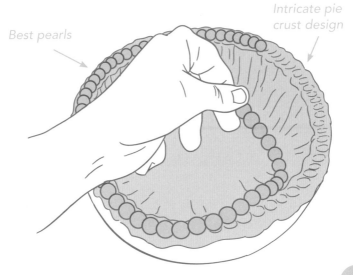

Intricate pie crust design

Best pearls

CHOCOLATE BOWLS

There are only so many ways you can dress up a scoop of ice cream to make it look fancy. But serving it in a chocolate bowl? That's a game-changer.

First, prepare a sheet of baking paper and put it to one side. Then blow up a balloon – size-wise it should sit comfortably in the palm of your hand. Next, melt a bar of chocolate in a heatproof bowl. Allow the chocolate to cool slightly (but keep stirring it so that it doesn't set) and dip the rounded top of the balloon into the chocolate. Place the balloon chocolate-side down onto the pre-prepared baking paper and leave it to set. Once the chocolate is hard, pop the balloon; you will be left with an edible bowl to impress your dinner party guests. And the best bit: there's no washing up.

Baking sheet

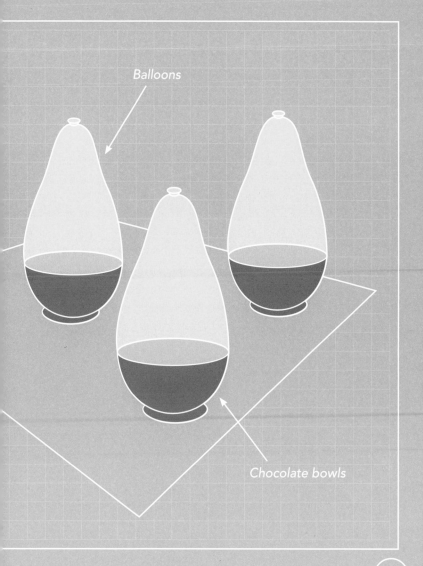

Balloons

Chocolate bowls

FREEZE TO FROST

Do you dream of being able to produce the kind of cakes you see in a shop window, with sharp, defined edges to their icing? Well, with this hack, you can!

The key is to frost your cake when it's nearly frozen. To freeze a cake, wrap it in a layer of cling film and a layer of foil before putting it in the freezer. When you're ready to ice, take it out of the freezer, remove all outer layers and allow it to thaw slightly. When a cake is cold, fewer crumbs will stray into your icing, and it holds its shape much better, meaning that you can a get a clean finish and those smooth, sharp edges much more easily.

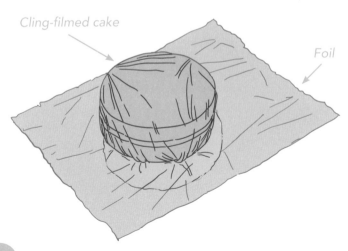

Cling-filmed cake

Foil

BAKE FROM THE HEART

Here at *Baking Hacks* HQ we firmly believe that the way to your heart is through your stomach. And what better way to seduce the object of your desire than with heart-shaped food?

All you need are a few marbles. Line your cupcake pan with cake cases as you usually would. Then slip a marble into each well in the tin. When you pour the batter into the tin, the marble will press one side of the cake inwards, and you'll be left with heart-shaped cakes. Irresistible.

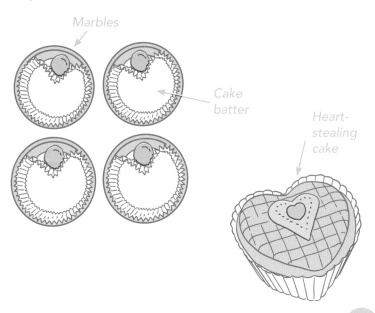

Marbles

Cake batter

Heart-stealing cake

CHOCOLATE DRIZZLING HACK

It is a truth universally acknowledged that anything covered in chocolate is a crowd-pleaser. Here's a hack to ensure you get the perfect consistency for dipping and drizzling every time.

Melt your chocolate as usual. Then, for every 175 g of chocolate you use, add approximately one tablespoon of coconut oil to the mixture. This will thin the chocolate very slightly, meaning that you can pour rather than dollop your chocolate wherever it needs to go. Dipping your biscuits and covering your cakes will be a breeze.

Chocolate with added coconut oil

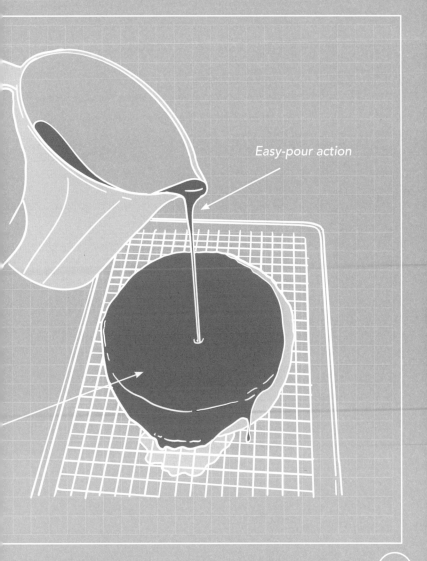

Easy-pour action

FAUX FONDANT

If you want to achieve the look of a fondant-iced cake without the time, effort and many kilos of fondant icing thrown away in failed attempts, read on.

Make a batch of buttercream icing, but use vegetable shortening instead of butter (if you bought some for the Magic Cake Release hack on p.83 you're winning). Cover your cake in buttercream icing as you usually would. Then take a good-quality paper towel and press it gently onto the top and sides of the cake. It will smooth the surface and leave you with that highly coveted fondant look.

I can't believe it's not fondant

Paper towel

SOPHISTICATED SAUCE

Nothing says 'this baker knows what they're doing' like a decorative swirl of sauce on a plate. It looks simple, but anyone who's ever tried to artfully smear their raspberry coulis with a spoon knows that it's easier said than done.

So try this hack next time you need to impress. Put your sauce into a clean, empty squeezy sauce bottle instead, and proceed to masterfully drip, trail and dab with ease.

Old sauce
bottle

Fancy
drizzling

MONEY-SAVING HACKS

There's a lot of fancy equipment out there. OK, so maybe you do need an oven, but do you really need cake cases? Cooling racks? A sieve? Of course not! Here are some tips to help you save your pennies but still bake like the best of them.

WINE BOTTLE ROLLING PIN

Never let a little thing like not having a rolling pin keep you from baking your favourite biscuits ever again.

A clean, empty wine bottle will do the job just as well.

Empty wine bottle

Dough

CUSTOMISE YOUR TRAY

Flummoxed by a recipe that, yet again, demands that you use a tray of obscure proportions that you don't have? Don't sweat it – hack it!

All you need is kitchen foil and a tray larger than the one you need. Take a long strip of foil and fold it so that it's the same height as your tray. Position the foil strip in the tray wherever you need it so that you're left with a space of the right dimensions for your bake.

Pastry

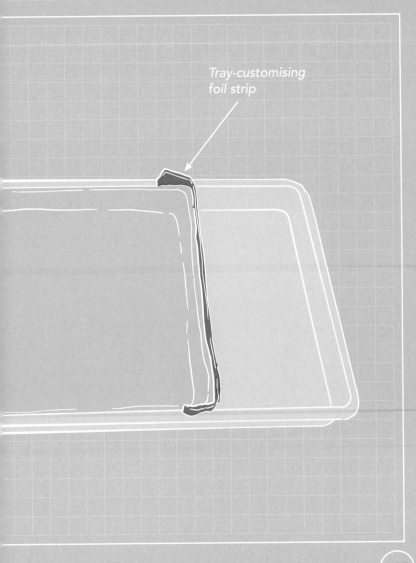

Tray-customising foil strip

FREE-STANDING CAKE

All your heart wants is to bake the fluffiest, tastiest blueberry muffins that your kitchen has ever seen, but all you have is a flat baking tray. Don't despair – a hack is on hand.

Instead of using one cake case per muffin, use three. Having multiple cake cases instead of just one will make the structure stronger and the cases will hold their shape without the aid of a muffin tin. You shall have muffins after all.

Tasty muffins

Three-layered cases

HOMEMADE CUPCAKE LINERS

If you've run out of cake cases, then all is certainly not lost. With this hack, you can still have your cake (and eat it), and it'll even look like it came from an expensive local bakery.

Simply cut squares of baking paper and push them down into the wells of the cake or muffin tin, making sure that the edges of each well are covered. Spoon your batter in, bake your cakes as normal and enjoy the admiration on peoples' faces as they partake of your artisanal goods.

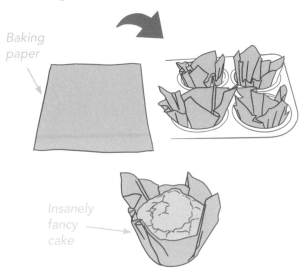

Baking paper

Insanely fancy cake

HOMEMADE PIPING BAG

You go to the cupboard and - horror of horrors - you've run out of piping bags. Little Jemima won't be impressed with her plain birthday cake this year...

Stay calm, because you can get the job done with a freezer bag instead. Just snip off one corner - either a small hole for precision icing, or a hole big enough for a nozzle - load the bag with icing (there's a helpful hack for that on p.109) and away you go.

Simple freezer bag

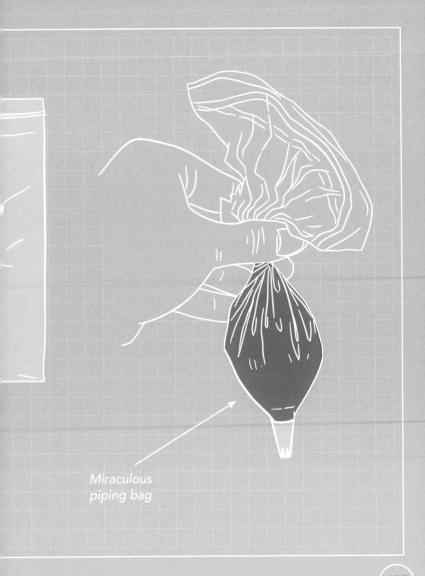

*Miraculous
piping bag*

COOKIE CUTTER #1

If ever you suddenly find yourself short of cookie cutters there's no need to panic. Keep your head and follow the *Baking Hacks* advice.

Instead of rolling your dough out flat, roll it into a sausage shape. The circumference should be the size that you want your biscuits to be. Then place the dough in the fridge for a few hours. Once chilled, cut the dough-sausage into slices to form your biscuits.

Biscuit dough

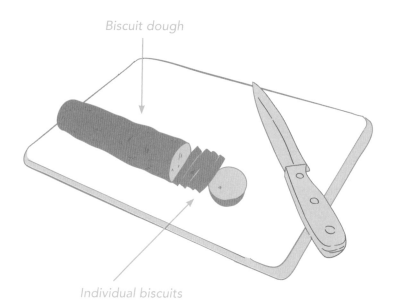

Individual biscuits

COOKIE CUTTER #2

If you're sceptical about the hack on p.128 and you'd rather stick to the good old-fashioned method of cutting your biscuits out with a cutter (but you still don't actually have one) then this hack is just the thing for you.

A clean, empty can with both ends removed can be used as a cookie cutter instead. You won't have as much flexibility with the size of your cookies, but you will at least have the satisfaction of punching out holes in your dough.

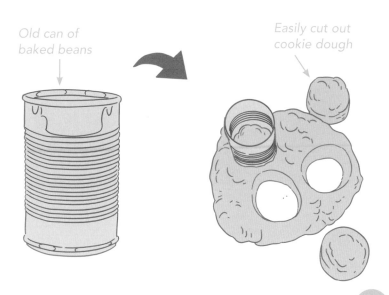

Old can of
baked beans

Easily cut out
cookie dough

COOKIE CUTTER #3

If your local kitchen shop doesn't have the obscurely shaped cutters that you need (honestly – what kind of kitchen shop are they?), I am here with the perfect solution.

Break out the aluminium foil and fold a long piece in half lengthways several times. Then bend the strip into whatever size or shape of cutter you need. The more firmly you're able to fold the foil the better, as you'll get a much cleaner shape. The world of biscuit shaping is your oyster.

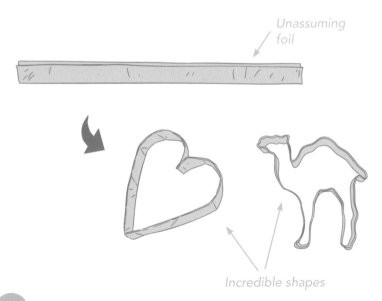

Unassuming foil

Incredible shapes

BLIND-BAKING HACK

The baking world is full of clever but essentially unnecessary items to help you bake. If your recipe advises you to use baking beans to blind bake your pastry – don't listen to them! Instead, take the *Baking Hacks* advice.

Blind bake your pastry with rice instead of shelling out for baking beans that you'll only use once in a blue moon. The rice is heavy enough to weigh down the baking paper and won't burn in the oven. Baking beans shmaking shmeans.

Rice

Baking paper

DISPOSABLE TIN

Using one of your own tins to bring goodies to the church cake sale is a rookie error. You can label it much as you want, but let it out of your sight for one minute and you're never going to see that tin again.

So make a disposable, recyclable one instead. Take an empty cereal box and tape it closed at the top and bottom. Then cut the large front panel away. Line it with baking paper, and you're all set to transport your signature brownies with ease, without having to worry about reclaiming your tin when they're all gone.

Trusty cereal box

Nifty brownie transporter

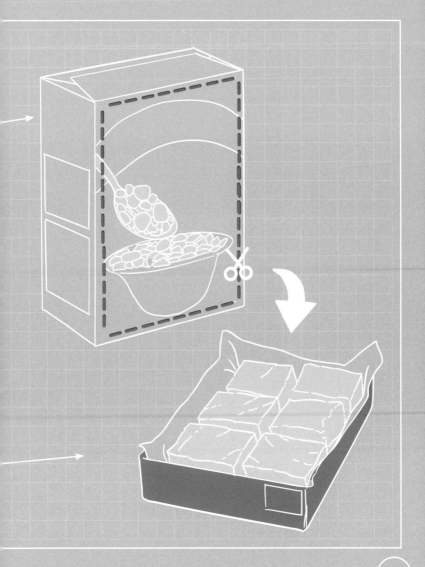

SIEVE ALTERNATIVE

To get light, airy cakes, it should come as no surprise that a key ingredient is, well, air. But how do you achieve this if you don't have a sieve?

Just use a whisk. Instead of sifting your flour through a sieve, add it straight to the bowl and stir it for a minute or so with a whisk – the larger the better. Not only will this aerate the flour, but it should keep your work surfaces tidier too. It's a win-win.

Hand whisk

Flour

DIY COOLING RACK

When you bake as much as I do, you run out of space on your cooling racks pretty quickly. Here's what I do when I need extra space to cool my bakes.

Take a muffin tin and turn it upside down on the counter. When you take your pie out of the oven simply put it on top of the tray. There will be enough space between the moulds to let the air circulate and for your bake to cool. This works best for larger dishes, such as pies, tarts or large cakes, but you may be able to balance something smaller, like cookies, across the moulds as well.

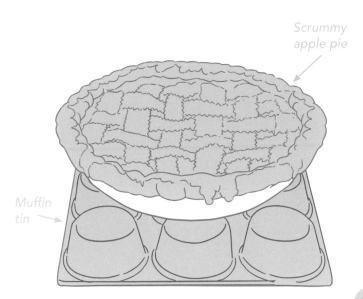

Scrummy
apple pie

Muffin
tin

DIY CHOCOLATE MOULD

Do you ever get the urge to create something small and intricate out of chocolate? I know I do. Here's an easy way to do it without having to scour the internet for a mould in the obscure shape of your choice.

Find a small container and fill it with brown sugar. The sugar should be fairly densely packed. Then take the item that you want to create out of chocolate and press one side of it into the sugar until the indentation of half of it is imprinted. Repeat for the other side of the object. Then carefully fill both the moulds with chocolate. When it's set, attach the two halves together, and your chocolate creation is complete.

Imprint to be filled with chocolate

Brown sugar

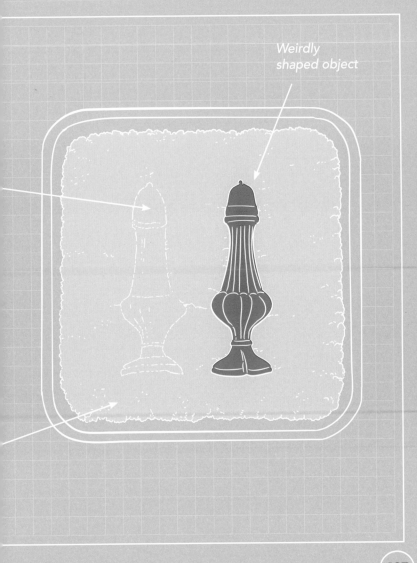

Weirdly shaped object

EDIBLE GLITTER

The motto, 'If in doubt, cover it with glitter' is applicable to many areas of life, but it's particularly relevant to baking. You don't have to fork out for it either – here's how to make your own.

Line a tray with baking paper. Put 100 g granulated sugar into a bowl, add half a tablespoon of liquid food dye and stir. Once the sugar is coated in dye, spread it evenly on the baking paper. Bake for 8–10 minutes at 180°C/gas mark 4 (if you see any sugar melting or boiling, it should come out of the oven). Allow the sugar to cool before sprinkling liberally or storing it in an airtight container.

Sugar

Coloured sugar on tray

Food colouring

Fabulous

NIFTY LEMON JUICER

If you don't have a fancy lemon juicer complete with little teeth to catch the pips, don't worry. You can still juice lemons with speed and ease.

Simply squeeze the lemon through a pair of tights (but make sure they're clean!). The material will be thin enough to let the juice through and will catch any pips making a bid for freedom.

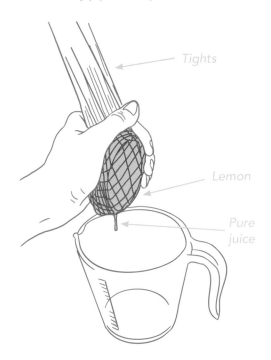

Tights

Lemon

Pure juice

FABULOUS FOAM

If you find yourself needing foamy, frothy milk and you don't have a device to help you do it, rest assured, because you don't need one!

For this hack, all you need is a jam jar with an airtight lid. Pour milk into the jar, taking care not to fill it more than halfway, and screw the lid on firmly. Then shake what your mama gave you (and the jar), until the milk has doubled in volume. As with the hack on p.70, this trick works best when both the milk and the jar are chilled.

Milk

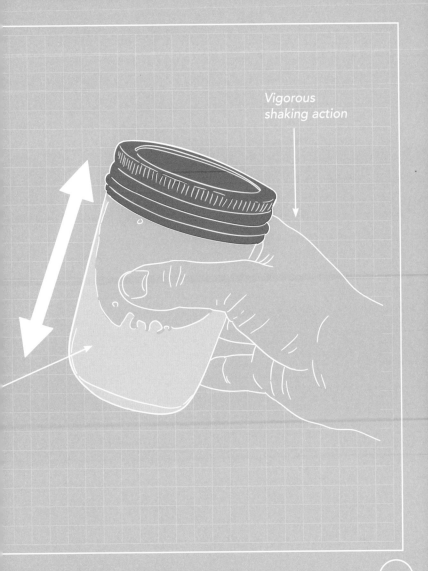

Vigorous shaking action

SPEED SLICER

At *Baking Hacks* HQ we believe that every second is precious, so we're especially pleased with this hack as it saves you at least three.

Don't waste time slicing strawberries with a knife like an average Joe. Use an egg slicer instead and make quick work of that fruit salad.

Egg
slicer

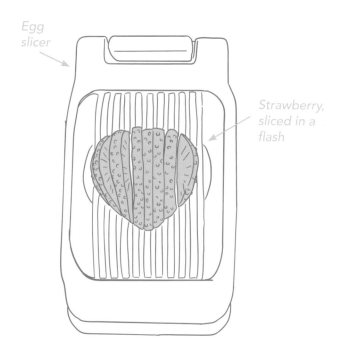

Strawberry,
sliced in a
flash

QUICK FIXES

A wise man once said, 'When you can't change the wind, adjust your sails.' At *Baking Hacks* we like to say, 'When you can't fix your bake, adjust your plan.' When disaster strikes you can stay cool with these next hacks.

BISCUIT RESCUE HACK

If you're midway through baking your biscuits and spy the beginnings of burnt edges through the door of the oven, act quickly, using this next hack!

Take the biscuits from the oven immediately. Transfer them onto a baking sheet (or just remove the sheet from the hot tray if they're already on one), and put them in the freezer for a few minutes. The sudden cold temperature will halt the baking process and stop the biscuits from cooking any more. Crisis averted.

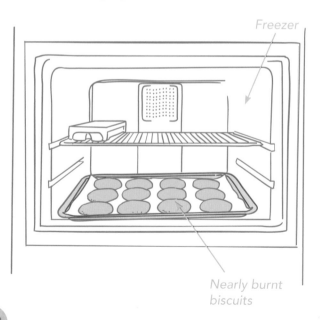

Freezer

Nearly burnt biscuits

BURNT BAKE REVIVER

You've fallen at the last hurdle; you left your muffins or cookies in the oven for a few minutes too long and now they're blackened around the edges. Before you throw them out, try this hack.

Take a fine-holed grater and gently grate away the singed edges. The parts under the burnt areas will be golden brown and nobody need ever know that you didn't set the timer.

Biscuit-
saving
grater

Burnt
biscuits

DRY CAKE HACK #1

If you didn't use the skewer hack on p.96 and have now ended up with a dry, over-baked cake, don't beat yourself up about it. Here's a hack instead.

Take a freezer bag large enough to contain your cake. Put your cake in it together with a slice of bread and leave it for a few hours. The cake will regain some of the moisture it lost in the oven by absorbing it from the bread. This is more of a temporary fix than a permanent one, so replace the bread regularly, or decorate and serve quickly!

Freezer bag

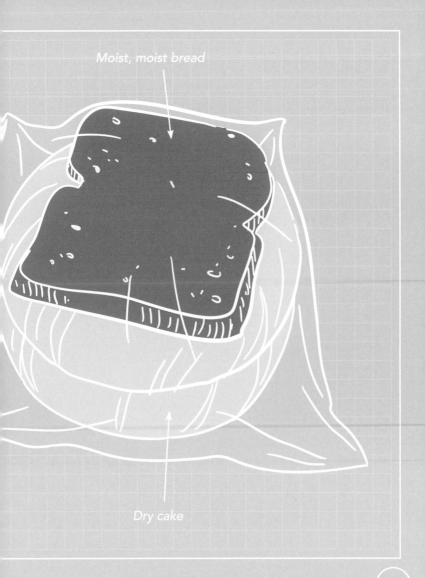

DRY CAKE HACK #2

With this next hack, a cake can be transformed from a scene of desiccation into a scene of delight.

Turn it from a regular cake into a drizzle cake. Boil sugar and water together to make a sugar syrup, adding in other flavours, such as lemon juice, if you want to spice things up. Then poke holes in the top of your dry cake with a fork or skewer and drizzle the syrup over the top. The dryness of the cake is perfect for absorbing the syrup. Baking mishap? More like baking win.

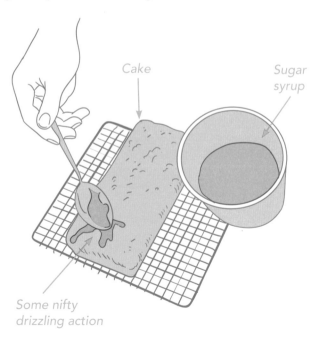

Cake

Sugar syrup

Some nifty drizzling action

DRY CAKE HACK #3

Here's another hack to save your over-baked cake.

Bring a saucepan of water to the boil. Put your dry cake on a cooling rack, and then put the rack on the top of the pan. Leave the cake to absorb the moisture from the steam for a couple of minutes before removing. As with the hack on p.146, this is more of a temporary solution, so try to serve your cake no more than a few hours after steaming.

Cake not so dry any more

Steam

Pan of hot water

DRY CAKE HACK #4

If you fear that your over-baked cake really is beyond revival, here's another hack to cover your tracks. Abandon the idea of one whole cake, and turn it into cake pops instead.

Crumble up your whole cake, either with your fingers or a food processor, and mix in cream cheese until it forms a dough. Roll it into balls, cover them in chocolate and you'll have delicious, bite-sized treats. You can even attach lollipop sticks to them for extra pizzazz. Of course this was your plan all along.

Crumbled cake

Beautiful cake pops

Cake, rolled into dough balls

SUNKEN CAKE HACK #1

Picture the scene: you've taken your cake from the oven only to find that it's sunk (just like your heart). But don't despair – there is an easy way to save the day.

Just use copious decoration to cover the mishap instead. Whether you use large decorative flowers, a thick layer of buttercream icing, or a sky-high pile of whipped cream and fruit, there's no easier way to hide a sunken middle. (Next time your cake is baking, don't open the oven door so much!)

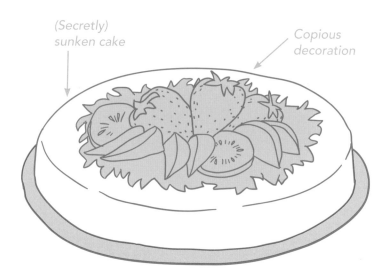

(Secretly)
sunken cake

Copious
decoration

SUNKEN CAKE HACK #2

If you've got a sunken cake on your hands and want to remove all trace of the unfortunate mishap, here's the perfect way to style it out.

Turn it into a ring cake instead. First, cut out the sunken middle section and dispose of the evidence. Then frost and decorate the cake that remains, and you'll have a centrepiece to be proud of.

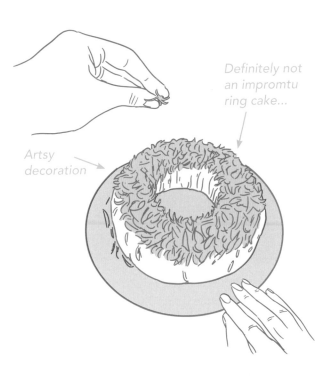

Definitely not an impromtu ring cake...

Artsy decoration

CAKE BUMP HACK

If your cake is looking more like Mount Fuji than Table Mountain, this simple hack is for you.

Take a bread knife (or a length of dental floss - see p.174) and level off the unsightly bump. Then flip the cake over and frost the base instead. Problem solved.

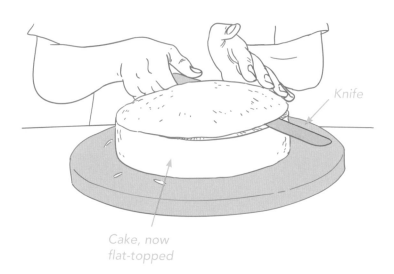

Knife

Cake, now flat-topped

BUNGLED BISCUITS

You tried to remove your biscuits from the sheet but they disintegrated in your hands and now you're left standing before a tray of tiny (albeit delicious) crumbs. All is not lost, however: there's a use for them yet!

Turn them into the topping for a crumble instead. Stew fruit as you normally would for a crumble, and pour it into an ovenproof dish. Then, instead of preparing the crumble topping, simply sprinkle your broken biscuits on top and bake.

Broken biscuit topping

Crumble of triumph

THE LAST RESORT

If things have gotten really dire, and none of the aforementioned hacks are going to save your cake then it's still not time to throw in the towel. *Baking Hacks* has one final suggestion for you.

Use the cake as a base for trifle. It doesn't matter if your cake is burnt, misshapen, dry, or all of the above. Just cut that baking catastrophe into pieces (trim off the blackest bits) and use them to line the bottom of a bowl. Layer fruit, jelly, custard and cream on the top, and nobody will ever know what happened before.

Utter failure of a bake

Show-stopping trifle

BAKING CHEATS

Some people call it cheating. We prefer to call it 'streamlining', 'creative thinking' or 'superb time management'. Whatever name it goes by, here are some great ways to get stellar bakes with minimum expenditure of time and effort.

SUPER-STRONG WHIPPED CREAM

When you make your pavlova you want it to look gosh darn fantastic. But if you've got whipped cream that's going to lose its shape after a day, this isn't going to happen. Here's a hack to guarantee that your cream stays stiff and strong.

The trick is to add marshmallow creme – this can be purchased cheaply in supermarkets. Whip 240 ml heavy cream until it has thickened slightly (but not so much that it can stand up on its own). Add 200 g marshmallow creme and continue whipping until you reach the consistency you want. Then top that pavlova: the cream will stand strong for at least three days.

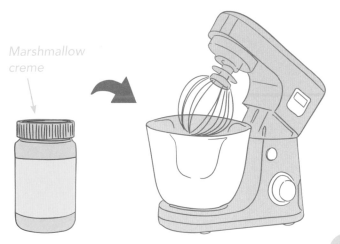

Marshmallow creme

TWO-INGREDIENT CAKE

Why should a little thing like not having any ingredients mean that you don't get cake? Here's a hack to furnish you with the good stuff in just two ingredients.

All you need is 500 ml melted ice cream and 150 g self-raising flour. Combine the two in a bowl until they're smooth. Then transfer to a loaf tin or cake pan, bake at 180°C/gas mark 4 for 45 minutes, and a cake is born. It doesn't get much easier than that.

ALL-PURPOSE FLOUR

Two-ingredient cake

BOXED CAKE HACK #1

Boxed cake mix is a dream when you're in a rush, but let's not kid ourselves: it doesn't taste as good as a cake made from scratch. So listen up, time-savers – this is a true baking cheat, and a useful one to have up your sleeve (or your apron) in times of need.

Just add an extra egg to the mixture, and the cake will taste homemade. Alternatively, pimp your cake mix easily by replacing the water with something else. Orange juice, coconut milk, coca cola... the possibilities are endless.

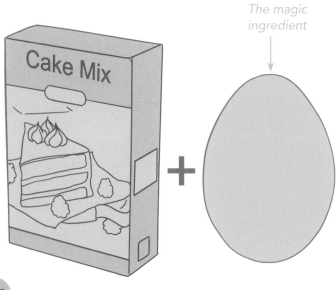

The magic ingredient

BOXED CAKE HACK #2

Here's another way to make your boxed mix taste less 'supermarket' and more 'artisan bakery'.

Replace the vegetable oil with melted butter, and your cake will enter a whole new world of fluffy, buttery goodness.

Melted butter

Cake mix

MAGIC MAYO

For those willing to take a leap of faith, here's a hack to guarantee that you'll never bake a dry cake ever again. But only if you can handle the truth.

Begin by making your cake as normal. Just before you add your dry ingredients to your batter, add three tablespoons of mayonnaise and combine. Before you shake your head in disgust, remember that mayonnaise is essentially eggs and oil – ingredients that will take the moistness of your cake to the next level. *Baking Hacks* tip: this hack works especially well on chocolate cakes.

Surprising cake-moisturising mayo

ORGANIC
MAYONNAISE

QUICK BISCUITS

If you want to go from zero to biscuits in under 20 minutes, listen up!

Take an average-sized pre-packaged cake mix (approximately 430 g) and put it into a bowl. Add two eggs and 120 ml vegetable oil (which is less liquid than you usually add to a boxed cake mix), and mix the whole lot together to create a dough. Roll the dough into balls, place on a lined baking tray, bake at 180°C/gas mark 4 for 8–10 minutes, and you're sorted.

The easiest biscuits ever

ONE-INGREDIENT ICE CREAM

I defy you to show me someone who isn't impressed when you announce that you're serving your 'homemade ice cream'. This time the joke's on them, because with this hack, it couldn't be easier.

All you will need are a few bananas (the exact quantity depending on how much ice cream you want). The riper they are, the better. Slice the banana into bite-sized pieces and blend them in a food processor for a few minutes. Then put your mashed banana into a sealable container and place in the freezer for a few hours. The result: rich, creamy, *healthy* ice cream!

Just banana. Amazing.

SNACK HACK

Are you looking for a tasty treat to whip up for the office party that requires no particular skill, forward planning, time or effort, that's healthy, vegan, gluten-free, dairy-free and also looks fantastic? Then thank goodness for this next hack.

Slice fruit into flat pieces and use cookie cutters to press out funky shapes. You and your colleagues can enjoy star-shaped melon pieces, flower-shaped kiwi or heart-shaped apple. Level up by combining your shapes: a flower-shaped piece of apple with half a grape balanced in the middle becomes a beautiful flower.

Standard slice of fruit

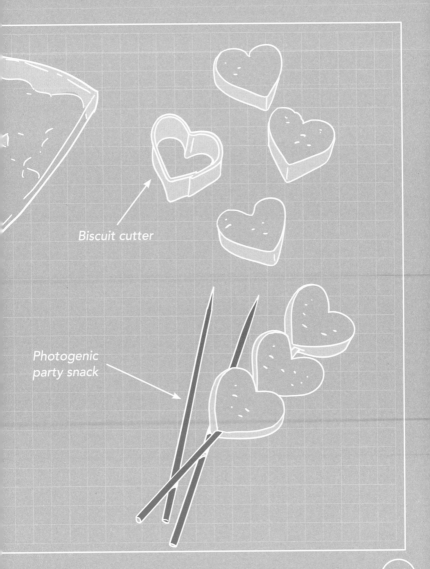

Biscuit cutter

Photogenic
party snack

PIPING GUIDE

If the thought of piping a design onto your cake freehand turns your legs to jelly, take a few deep breaths and read this next hack.

Take a toothpick and lightly mark out your course before you begin. If you make a mistake, just smooth over the icing and try again, and when you come to piping the real thing you'll just be joining the dots. Your steady hand and eye for design will be the talk of the town.

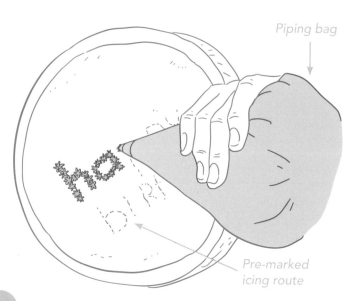

Piping bag

Pre-marked icing route

SUPER-QUICK FROSTING

If you've got ten minutes to get from kitchen to cake sale, your cupcakes are still in the oven, and you can't face the idea of presenting naked, undecorated cake to the masses, then this hack is for you.

When your cakes have five minutes left to bake, grab a bag of marshmallows and pop one on top of each cake. By the time they're done the marshmallow will be soft enough to spread. Your cakes will be coated in a soft, gooey, delicious topping, and their modesty, and your baking reputation, will be preserved.

Marshmallows

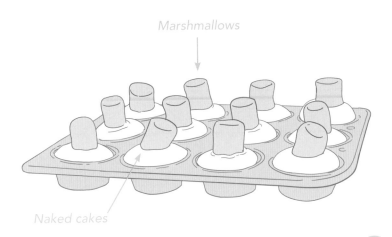

Naked cakes

TWO-TONE SWIRL ICING

Nothing says 'accomplished baker' like two-tone buttercream icing on top of a cupcake. But you've heard that this is a particularly tricky technique, right? Wrong! Not with the help of this hack.

Make your two colours of icing as you normally would. Then put one lot in one piping bag, and the other in a second bag. Then take a third bag, and prepare it with a nozzle. Put both the filled piping bags inside the third bag, push them to the end, and pipe away! Your colours will be kept clear and distinct, and you'll get that two-tone swirl with minimal fuss.

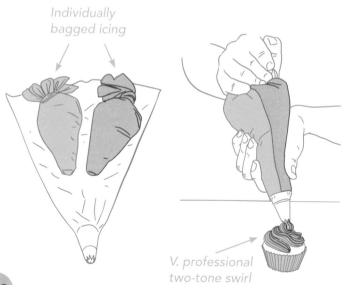

Individually bagged icing

V. professional two-tone swirl

MISCELLANEOUS HACKS

Impromptu biscuit carrier? But of course. Picture-perfect cake slices? Easy. Pristine pancakes? No problem. The hacks in this next chapter are the kind that are best served when whipped out at opportune moments to impress friends, family and colleagues.

NO-STRESS LAYER CAKE

Cutting a cake in half to make a layer cake is a risky business: one wrong move and you'll be serving up a plate of wonky cake and disappointment. Say goodbye to the grief of misshapen layers with this easy hack.

Take a length of unflavoured dental floss, long enough to wrap around your cake at least one and a half times. Wrap the floss around the circumference of your cake where you want it to split. Then gently pull the dental floss tight. Like cheese-wire, it will cut straight through your cake and you'll end up with two perfectly level layers. Smashing.

Unflavoured dental floss

Large cake,
nearly two
smaller cakes

BUTTER REJUVENATOR

If you've been over-enthusiastic with the microwave and you've bypassed 'softened' and gone straight to 'extremely squishy' on the butter pliancy scale, the solution is just a hack away.

Put your wilting butter into a small bowl, then place that bowl into a larger one. Add some ice cubes and cold water to the bigger bowl, and give your butter an ice bath until it hardens up again.

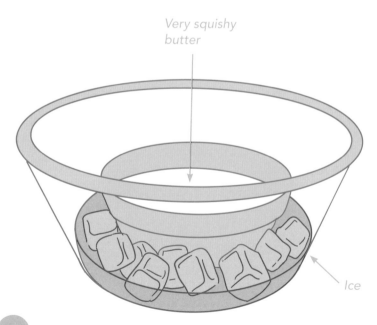

Very squishy butter

Ice

MESS-FREE PANCAKES

To get a rainbow you have to put up with the rain. Similarly, if you want pancakes you've got to put up with the mess, as batter has a tendency to slop and drip over your nice clean kitchen. Or do you?

Next time you're making pancakes, take a clean, empty sauce bottle and decant your pancake mixture into it. Now, instead of ladling that sloppy batter over your kitchen counter, you can simply squeeze the mixture straight into the pan.

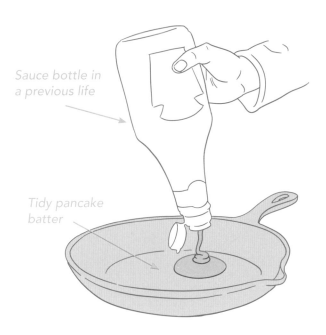

Sauce bottle in
a previous life

Tidy pancake
batter

CAKE TRANSPORTER

It's all well and good creating a beautiful masterpiece of a cake, but things get tricky when you need to transport it anywhere. Here's a hack to get it from A to B intact and unsullied.

Take several pieces of uncooked spaghetti and poke them around the top edge of your cake. They should be angled so that their tips are facing outwards slightly. Then take a long piece of cling film and gently drape it over the spaghetti. Your cake will be protected from the elements (or prying fingers) and the spaghetti will ensure that the cling film doesn't cling to the cake.

Spaghetti ⟶

Cling film ⟶

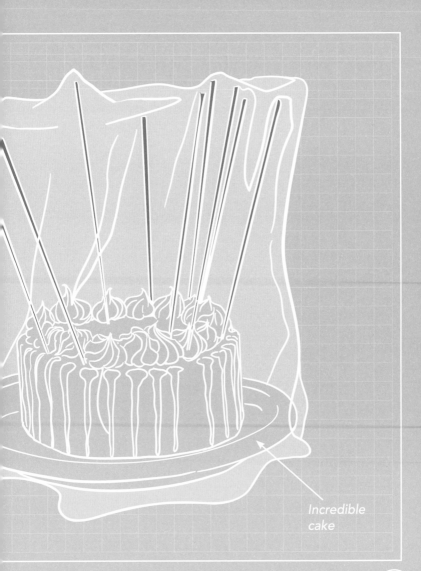

Incredible cake

COOKIES ON DEMAND

If you're often called on to bake cookies at the drop of a hat, here's a hack that's worth deploying in advance.

Begin by making double the quantity of cookie dough that you normally would. Bake half of it as normal. Then, with the other half, form the dough into balls, put them into a sealable freezer bag, and freeze them. When the next time comes for cookies, simply take the pre-prepared dough from the freezer and bake. There's no need to defrost them, but you may have to add an extra minute or two onto the baking time. Dough can be stored for three months in the freezer.

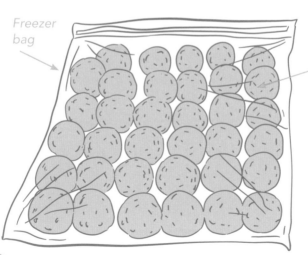

Freezer bag

Biscuit dough, ready for action

QUICK CRUMBS

Here's a quick and easy way to get those biscuits crushed for your cheesecake.

Put your biscuits into a clear plastic food bag, then seal, making sure that there isn't any air trapped inside making the bag inflate. Then take a rolling pin (or wine bottle, see p.121) and use it to crush the biscuits into tiny crumbs – no food processor required.

Biscuits

Freezer bag

EXTRA-CHOCOLATEY BROWNIES

Everybody claims to be able to make a good brownie, but this hack will make you stand out from the crowd.

Mix a teaspoon of instant coffee granules with a tablespoon of warm water, and mix this into your brownie batter before you put it into the tin. You won't be able to taste the coffee but it has the effect of enhancing the chocolatey flavour, giving you killer brownies every time.

Coffee granules

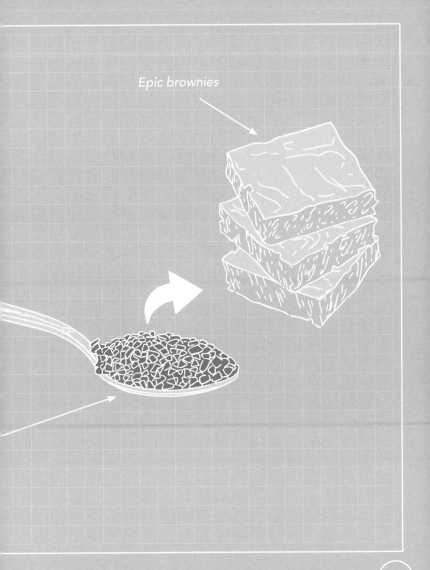

Epic brownies

DIY BISCUIT HOLDER

No matter how nicely you arrange them, biscuits always look anticlimactic sitting in a box all piled on top of one another. So here's a way to style them up.

For this hack, all you need is a paper plate. Make two cuts in the top and bottom, as shown in image 1. Then fold down the lines marked in image 2. Tape the sides, and you've got yourself a sweet biscuit carrier to show off your cookies.

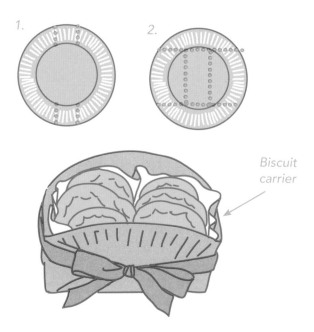

1.

2.

Biscuit carrier

DIY CUPCAKE HOLDER

Making cupcakes always seems like a good idea until you have to transport them anywhere. Here's a hack to make sure your icing stays unsmudged and your cakes stay upright in transit.

Take two large disposable plastic cups and trim the tops off so that they are approximately 6 cm in height. Place a cupcake in the bottom of one cup, place the second cup on top of the first, and secure the two halves with tape. Repeat for as many cakes as you have and transport them in comfort and style.

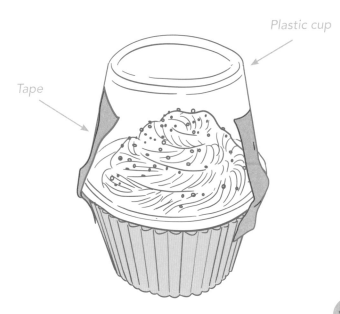

Plastic cup

Tape

PERFECT SLICES

If dental floss isn't your cup of tea (or perhaps you've only got the mint-flavoured stuff in your cupboard) there's still a chance for you to get Instagram-perfect edges to your bakes when you cut them.

Take your knife and warm the metal by running it under hot water for a few seconds. Dry the knife and then, while it's still warm, use it to cut your cake or slice your brownies. Depending on how many slices you're cutting, you may need to re-warm your knife a few times.

Hot
water

Knife

FINAL WORD

Congratulations – you are now a baking hacks hero! Whatever drama the kitchen throws at you, you've got the know-how to tackle it with the calm smile of someone who has everything completely under control. You'll go far, my friend.

Feel free to pass on these nuggets of genius to fellow bakers, and if you have some baking hacks that aren't featured in the book but deserve to be in print, email them to auntie@summersdale.com

Until next time – get baking!

HACKS INDEX

BEAUTY
HACKS

Make-up Cheats, Skincare Tricks
and Styling Tips

Aggie Robertson

ISBN: 978 1 84953 574 8

£9.99

**Do you wake up in the morning and think, 'I wish
there was a quicker way to put on my make-up?'**

**Do you find yourself getting so frustrated at nail
varnish smudges that you've given up even trying?**

**Do you hate spending your hard-earned money on hair
and beauty products, but still enjoy expressing your style?**

These and dozens of other hair, skincare, nail and make-up
dilemmas are solved with this compendium of ingenious
BEAUTY HACKS. This fully illustrated manual covers everything
from DIY face masks and time-saving make-up cheats to quick
and easy styling tips – everything you need to look good, feel
good, and still have time for the other fun things in life!

If you're interested in finding out more about
our books, find us on Facebook at
Summersdale Publishers
and follow us on Twitter at
@Summersdale.

WWW.SUMMERSDALE.COM